# Training Children

## in

# Godliness

**Written by** Jacob Abbott
**Revised and Edited by** Michael J. McHugh

*Train up a child in the way he should go: and
when he is old, he will not depart from it.*
*Proverbs 22:6*

· A PUBLICATION OF ·

*Christian Liberty Press*

502 West Euclid Avenue, Arlington Heights, Illinois 60004

This work is dedicated to the memory of Jacob Abbott, an nineteenth century educator, minister, and author, whose writings formed the basis of this book.

Editor:  Michael J. McHugh
Typesetter:  Eric L. Pfeiffelman

Chapter five of this text was originally published in an expanded form
under the title: *The Principle of Biblical Charity* (Jacob Abbott, © 1989,
Christian Liberty Press).

THE FIRST WRONG ACT.

# —Table of Contents—

# About the Author

Jacob Abbott was born in Holloway, Maine on November 14, 1803, and died on October 31, 1874. During his lifetime, Abbott received universal acclaim as an evangelical minister, educator, and author. However, it was the gift of writing that provided Abbott with his greatest influence and fame.

As a writer of over 200 books, Abbott's great love was children's literature. He was considered by many to be the foremost writer of juvenile literature during his time. Historians describe Abbott as a kindly devout man from Puritan ancestry who was gifted with a spirit of gentleness, simplicity, and industry. In his modest way he typified the Puritan heritage at its simple best.

The book *Training Children in Godliness* is mostly comprised of choice selections of writing by Jacob Abbott on the subject of child training. In an effort to make the writings of Abbott more practical and enjoyable to today's reader, this book was recomposed and updated; with changes being made by the revisor for the sake of clarity and modern application. The revisor has been careful to leave the original intent of the author's writings intact during the process of revision and editorial activity.

This book was compiled, revised, and edited by Michael J. McHugh.

Mr. McHugh has worked in the field of Christian education for over fifteen years with the Christian Liberty Academy of Arlington Heights, Illinois. During his time with the Academy, Mr. McHugh has worked as a teacher, administrator, curriculum director, and textbook author.

As a father of three children, Mr. McHugh lives in the Chicago area where he is active as a deacon in an independent Reformed Protestant church — the Church of Christian Liberty.

# Preface

This book is designed to give parents, and other concerned adults, a thorough understanding of how to minister to the hearts of children.

We live in a day and age where parents are constantly bombarded with the need to fulfill the materialistic needs of their children. Now, meeting the physical needs of children is important; however, more parents should be challenged to evaluate their priorities in the area of child rearing. The most important aspect of raising children is to minister to their spiritual needs. As Jesus once said, "What does it profit a man if he gain the whole world and lose his own soul?"

Sadly, many parents have never fully understood that the God-ordained institution of the family is designed to provide parents with a spiritual ministry to the young. The "me-first" generation of twentieth-century America has forgotten the responsibility it has to prepare the next generation for godly dominion. God has assigned us a double-duty to perform while we remain on earth. First, to use the world in a Christ-like manner, while we continue in it; and, second, to prepare a generation to receive the trust, when we shall pass away from the scene. We are not only to occupy well ourselves, but to train up and qualify our successors.

It is my prayer that this book will enlighten and challenge both Christian parents and concerned adults to take full advantage of the opportunities God provides to turn the hearts of children in the way of righteousness.

Michael J. McHugh

THE FORCE OF EXAMPLE.

# Chapter 1

## How to Influence Children in Godliness

Chapter one is founded upon the simple fact that children normally pay more attention to what adults do, rather than to what they say. This fact should not lead us to believe, however, that what we say to children, or how we formally instruct them is unimportant. Rather, this point simply emphasizes the futility of trying to lead little ones to God through formal instruction only, while our personal witness remains cold and morally inconsistent.

The key to gaining positive access to a child's heart is through godly actions and godly teaching. In other words, our actions and words must compliment one another if we truly expect to make a wholesome impression on young people.

> "It is not the will of your Father which is in heaven, that one of these little ones should perish." Matthew 18:14

Suppose that a hundred healthy infants, each a few weeks old, were taken from the city of Chicago and arranged under the care of nurses in a suite of apartments. In an adjoining range of rooms let another hundred, taken from the most virtuous families in Scotland, be placed. Take another hundred from the high nobility of the families of England, and another from the lowest and most degraded haunts of vice, in the ghettos of Paris, France.

Now, if such an infantile representation were made of some of the most dissimilar of the classes into which the human race has been divided, and the children were brought together into the same apartment, the question is whether the most minute and thorough scrutiny could distinguish between the classes and assign each to its origin. They are to be under one common system of arrangement and attendance, and we have supposed all the subjects to be healthy in order to cut off grounds of distinction, which an intelligent physician might observe in hereditary tendencies to disease. Under these circumstances, if the several collections of infants were subjected to the most thorough examination, would any ingenuity or science be able to establish a distinction between them? Probably not. There would be the same forms, the same instincts, the same cries. The cradles which would lull the inmates of one apartment to sleep would be equally lulling to the others, and the same bright objects, or distinct sounds, which would awaken the senses and give the first gentle stimulus to mind, in one case, would do the same in all. Thus, inspection alone of these infants would not enable us to label them. And if they were to remain months or even years under our care, for concealed and embryo differences to be developed, we would probably wait in vain.

But instead of waiting, let us suppose that the four hundred children are dismissed, each to its mother and its home, and that they all pass through the years of childhood and youth, exposed to the various influences which surround them in the dwellings and neighborhoods to which they respectively belong – among the alleys and tall buildings of the city of Chicago, or the glens and hill sides of Scotland, or in the nurseries and drawing rooms of Grovesnor Square, or the dark crowded alleys of the Parisian faubourg. Distribute them thus to the places to which they respectively belong and leave them there until the lapse of time has brought them to maturity, then bring them all together for examination again.

How widely will they be found to have separated now? Though they commenced life under similar circumstances, their paths began at once to diverge. Now, when we compare them, they seem totally dissimilar. Contrast the Chicagoan with the Scot, the effeminate nobleman with the common criminal. Examine their characters thoroughly, their feelings, their opinions, their principles of conduct, their plans of life, their pursuits, their hopes, their fears. Almost everything is dissimilar. There is, indeed, a common humanity in all, but everything not essential to the very nature of man is changed; and characters are formed, so totally dissimilar, that we might almost doubt the identity of the species.

There is another thing to be observed, too. Every individual of each class, with scarcely a single exception, goes with his class and forms a character true to the influences which have operated upon him in his own home. You will look in vain for a character of luxurious effeminacy among the criminals' sons, or for virtuous principle among children brought up in a community of thieves. You can find cases enough of this kind, it is true, in works of fiction, but few in real life. So the Parisian children all become Frenchmen in their feelings and opinions, and principles of action; the aristocratic children all become aristocratic; and all those who in London or Paris find their homes in the crowded quarters of vice – if they are brought up thieves and beggars, thieves and beggars they will live.

And yet it is not education, in the common sense of that term, which produces these effects upon human character; that is, it is not formal efforts on the part of parents and friends to instruct and train up the young to walk in their own footsteps. In respect to the acquisition of knowledge and of accomplishments, great effort would be made to give formal instruction by some of the classes enumerated above. But in regard to almost all that relates to the formation of character, principles of action, the sentiments, and the feelings, the work is done by the thousand nameless influences which surround every child and which constitute the moral atmosphere in which he spends his youthful years.

Although each class of youngster began life with a sinful nature, the moral atmosphere that each child was exposed to in his home ultimately established the specific sinful patterns or tendencies that each child would be prone to follow.

Now everyone does a great deal to produce this kind of moral atmosphere, which is so central in determining the character of children who grow up in the midst of it. So much so that our influence upon the young is an exceedingly important part of our witness for Jesus Christ. In fact, God has assigned us a double duty to perform while we remain here. First, to use the world well, while we continue in it; and secondly, to prepare a generation to receive the trust when we shall pass away from the scene. We are not only to occupy well ourselves, but to train up and qualify our successors.

Perhaps the reader may think that these remarks on the subject of the young must be intended principally for parents. Far from it, for there are many relations in life which give us a very free access to the young, and an influence over them as an inevitable result. One person is a parent who consequently exercises a very controlling influence over the whole character and future prospects of his children. Another is a brother or sister who enjoys opportunities of influence almost as great as those of a father or mother. Still another may live in a family where there are no children, yet he is familiar with the families of neighbors or friends. He is thus thrown into frequent conversations with cousins and nephews and nieces, who are all the time catching his spirit and imitating his principles. An uncle or an aunt in such a case, is very apt to imagine that they have nothing to do but to keep in the good graces of their little relatives through an occasional picture book or toy. They forget the vast effects which ten years of almost constant and yet unguarded fellowship must have, in giving a right moral turn to the sentiments and the feelings of a child's heart. If we look back to our own early days, we shall remember in how many instances our opinions, sentiments, feelings, and perhaps our whole character was based upon the influence of an uncle, an aunt, or a neighbor.

In my father's family, there was an antique diary. It was the admiration of our childish eyes: a collection of college compositions, journals, and letters of an amiable uncle who died so early that his nephews could never know him, except through these remains. Many a rainy day and many a winter evening this diary was explored as a mine of instruction and enjoyment. Moral principle was awakened and cultivated by the sentiments of an essay; ambition was aroused by the spirit of a discussion; feelings of kindness and good will were cherished by the amiable and gentle spirit which breathed in the letters of the journal. This all undoubtedly exerted a vast influence by giving form to the character and sentiments of the boys who had access to it. How vastly greater would have been the influence of a constant fellowship with the living man.

Or, if the reader has neither of the above means of influence, he may be, perhaps, a Sunday school teacher, or he may have boys in his employment and have frequent contact with many youngsters who stand by unnoticed and listen to his directions or conversation. Thus we have, in a thousand other ways, a connection with the young which, though we may consider it slight, still exerts a powerful influence in impressing our characters upon the plastic material which it reaches. Hence, all who wish to do good should understand something of the character and susceptibilities of children, and make it a part of their constant care to exert as happy and as righteous an influence upon them as they can.

I proceed to give some practical directions by which this must be done. They are not intended solely for parents, but for all who have any contact with the young. Those who have made this topic a particular subject of reflection will find nothing new in these suggestions. They are the principles which common sense and common observation establish. They are presented here, not as discoveries but as obvious truth, to be kept in mind by those who would accomplish the most extensive and the most unmixed good in this part of the widely extended vineyard of God. We scarcely need remark that this chapter will relate solely to the employment of human means, which can only be successful in promoting that thorough change in the desires and affections of the heart which constitutes salvation, if they are in harmony with the will of God. One person plants, another waters, but it is God who gives the increase.

The plan of discussion which we shall pursue will be as follows:

I. To consider some of the prominent characteristics of childhood, in accordance with which an influence over the young can alone be secured

II. Deduce from them some general rules for ministering to the hearts of children

III. Prominent characteristics of childhood

To understand the course which must be taken in order to secure an influence over children, we must first understand the leading principles and characteristics of childhood, for it is these upon which we are to act. Let us summarize these principles: to exercise upon every object their dawning faculties, both of body and mind; to learn all they can about the world into which they are ushered, presenting as it does, so strange and imposing a spectacle to their senses; to love those who sympathize with and aid them in their objectives; and to catch the spirit and imitate the actions of those whom they thus love. These are the great leading principles by which the moral and intellectual nature of childhood is governed. These we shall consider in detail.

## To exercise their opening faculties.

The infant's first pleasure of this kind is the employment of the senses, beginning with gazing at the fire or listening with quiet pleasure to the sound of his mother's voice singing in his ear. While the little child just ushered into existence lies still in his cradle how often does the mother say, "I would like to know exactly what he is thinking of; what state of mind he is in." It is probably not very difficult to tell. Imagine yourself in his situation: look at a white wall and banish all thought and reflection, as far as you can, so as in imagination to arrest all operations of the mind, and retain nothing but vision. Let the light come into the eye and produce the sensation of whiteness, and nothing more. Let it awaken no thought, no reflection, no inquiry. Imagine yourself never having seen any white before, so as to make the impression a novel one, and also imagine yourself never having seen anything or heard anything before, so as to cut off all grounds for wonder or surprise. In a word, conceive of a mind in the state of simple sensation, with none of those thousand feelings and thoughts which sensation awakens in the spirit that is mature, and you probably have the exact state of the infantile intellect, when the first avenues are opened, by which the external world is brought to act upon its embryo mind. Can it be surprising then, under such circumstances, that even mere sensation should be pleasure?

As the child advances through the first months of existence, the mental part of the processes which the sensations awaken are more and more developed: for we are not to consider the powers of mind as called at once into existence, complete and independent at the beginning, but as gradually developed in the progress of years, and that too, in a great measure through the instrumentality of the senses. After some months have passed away, the impressions from without penetrate, as it were, farther within, and awaken new susceptibilities which gradually develop themselves. Now each new faculty is a new possession, and the simple exercise of it, without end or aim, is and must be a great positive pleasure. First comes the power to walk. We are always surprised at seeing how much delight the child, who first finds that he has strength and steadiness to go upright across the room, finds in going across again and again, from table to chair and from chair to sofa, as long as his strength remains. But why should we be surprised at it? Suppose the inhabitants of any town should find themselves suddenly possessed with the power of flying. We should find them for hours and days filling the air, flying from tree to tree and from house top to steeple, with no end or aim but the pleasure enjoyed in the simple exercise of a new power. The crowds which press to the ticket office of a new railroad, or the multitudes of delighted citizens brought out by an unexpected fall of snow in a warm climate, jingling about in every sort of vehicle that can be made to slide, show that man has not outgrown the principle.

Now this love of the exercise of the new power is obvious enough in the cases to which I have referred: seeing, hearing, walking, and in many other cases, as using the limbs – producing sound by striking hard bodies, breaking, upsetting, piling up blocks, or dragging about chairs. It is precisely the same feeling which would lead a man to go about uprooting trees or breaking enormous rocks, if he should suddenly find himself endued with the power of doing so. It is obvious enough, in these common physical operations, but we forget how many thousand mental processes there are, and others partly mental and partly physical, which possess the same charm and which in fact, make up a large portion of the occupations and enjoyments of childhood.

One of the earliest examples of a mental process which the

child is always pleased to exercise is understanding language. This may be described more accurately as the susceptibility of having pleasant images awakened in the mind by means of the power of certain sounds striking upon the ear. There are thousands who have observed the indications of this pleasure, who do not understand the nature and the source of it. Every mother, for example, observes that children love to be talked to, long before they can talk themselves. They imagine that what pleases the listener is his interest in the particular thing said, whereas it is probably only his interest in finding himself possessed of the new and strange power of understanding sounds. The mother says, "Where's Father? Where's Father?" and imagines that the child is pleased with the inquiry, whereas the infant is only pleased with that sound. It is this power of a word to produce a new and peculiar mental state which is probably the source of pleasure. Hence, the interest which the little auditor will take will not be in proportion to the point of the story, but to the frequency of the words contained in it which call up familiar and vivid ideas. It is not, therefore, what is understood but the mere power of understanding, the first development of a new mental faculty, which pleases the possessor.

Telling short stories is one of the simplest cases of the pleasure arising from the first exercise of a mental power. There are a thousand others which come forth, one after another, all through the years of childhood, and keep the young mind supplied with new sources of enjoyment. The amusements of children almost all derive their charm from their calling into exercise these dawning powers and enabling them to realize their possession. Digging in the ground, making little gardens, dressing a doll, playing store, playing soldier, and a thousand other things, call into play the memory, the imagination, the use of the limbs and senses, and thus exercise all the powers which have not yet lost their novelty. In fact, these powers are so rapidly progressive that they are always new.

This love of action is among the strongest of the propensities of childhood. It is certainly stronger than the appetites. In one case, I addressed a five year old boy, one at least as great a lover of candy and sweets as other boys his age, who had come into my study:

"Suppose I should tell you that you may either have four large sugar cookies, or you may go and get some sticks and paper to help me make a fire in the fireplace. Which would you rather do?"

"Why, I think I would rather help you make the fire," said the boy.

"Well, suppose I should tell you I was going to cut some paper into small pieces and wrap up a little of my kindling in each piece, and that you might have your choice: either to sit at the table and help me, or have a large piece of apple pie and a chocolate rabbit?"

The countenance of the child showed for an instant that it was a very serious question, but as he glanced an eye at the single pair of slender paper shears which lay upon the table he said, "I would rather help cut up the paper, if there are scissors enough." I have no doubt that a vast majority of children, from three to five years of age, would answer similar questions in a similar manner. What time and money are spent in sweets and expensive toys, to win an access to children's hearts, or to make them happy, while all the time the path to childish affection and enjoyment lies in so totally different a direction!

Anyone who will make childhood a study by observing its peculiarities and making experiments upon its feelings and tendencies, will find innumerable examples of the gratification they thus derive from the mere exercise of their dormant abilities. For example, there is enumeration, the power of conceiving numbers and their relations to one another. You may try this experiment. Take a young child, from three to four years of age, just old enough to begin to count, and sit with him at a table with ten buttons or kernels of corn before you. Let him look at the objects until his interest in them simply as objects is satisfied, and then begin to count them in various ways, so as gently to exercise his dawning powers of calculation. First count them all. Then count two of them, and two more, and then the remaining six. Go on perhaps thus:

"There is one, and there is another, that makes two; now there is another. How many do two and another, counted together, make? Let us see. One, two, three. They make three. Two things, and then another thing put with them, makes three things.

"Now we will put them in a row, and begin at this end and count them. It makes ten. Now we will begin at the other end, and see if it makes the same. Yes, it makes ten. It is the same. If we count them from this end to that end it makes ten, and if we count them from that end to this, it also makes ten. Now we will begin in the middle."

I state this to show how extremely short and simple the steps are which must be taken to enable the child to follow along. Such steps may be indefinitely varied with a little ingenuity, while the mind of the child is all the time occupied with simply reckoning numbers (i.e.: exercising an ability which he then, almost for the first time, finds that he possesses). In fact, he can hardly be said to have possessed it before. The exercise not merely calls them into play, it almost calls them into being. Go on with the exercise for the purpose of seeing how long he will continue to be interested. Unless some other object of excitement has possession of his mind, your patience will be exhausted long before he will be ready to stop.

Such examples are numberless. In fact, let an intelligent observer, when he sees children busily engaged in some scheme of amusement or occupation, pause a moment and look over them and ask, "What now is the secret source of pleasure here? What constitutes the charm? What power of body or mind is it, whose exercise here gives the enjoyment?" Such inquiries, and the analysis to which they lead, will give one a deep insight into the character and feelings of childhood and the great springs of its action. He who would gain an ascendancy over children must thus study them and aid them in this their leading desire. Make work for them, lay before them objects and occupations which shall make them acquainted with their abilities by calling them out into action, and lead them to a mode of action which will not interfere with the comforts or rights of others. No one can really understand children in this respect, sympathize with them, and aid them, without finding their hearts soon bound to him by the strongest ties of gratitude and affection. But we must pass on to the other leading principles of childhood previously listed.

**To learn all they can about the world into which they find themselves ushered.**

Next to their desire to act, their strongest impulse is a desire to know. This, like the other, has been universally observed; but, like the other, its true nature is not very exactly understood. It is not so much a desire to know what is remarkable or curious, as to know what is. It is the interest of knowing rather than an interest in the extraordinariness of what is known. All things are new to them; consequently, if you tell or explain something to them, it is of little consequence what it is.

Many parents have said, "My child is continually asking for stories, more stories, until my powers of imagination and invention are exhausted. What shall I do?" It shows that the parent who makes it does not distinctly understand the nature of the intellectual desire which he is called upon to supply. "Stories" mean talk, or at least any talk about what is new will satisfy the appetite for stories. Set off, then, on any tract and talk. Suppose you yourself could meet a man who had been on the moon, and he should sit down and describe accurately and vividly what he saw there one day – how he took a walk, what objects he saw, and what incidents he met with. Or suppose he should describe the interior of a room, any room whatever – the furniture, the instruments, their uses and construction. Why, there would not be an hour of his residence on the planet that would not afford abundant materials for a conversation to which we would listen with the deepest interest and pleasure. Well, now we must remember that this world is all moon to children, and we can scarcely go amiss in describing it. There is no hour in your day, and no object that you see, which is not full of subjects of interest to them.

Thus every object is the subject for a lecture or a story. A pin, a button, a key, a stick of wood – there is nothing which is not full of interest to children, if you will only be minute enough. Take a stick of wood. Tell how the tree it came from sprung up out of the ground years ago; how it grew every summer by the sap; how this stick was first a little bud, next year a shoot, and by and by a strong branch; how a bird perhaps built her nest on it; how squirrels ran up and down, and ants crept over it; how the woodman cut down the tree. Expand all the particulars into the most minute narrative. It is amazing that many parents complain that they are at a loss for subjects of conversation with their children.

If you describe nothing in your story which the child did not know before he will still enjoy the description. Our readers will not dispute this, if they call to mind the fact that the most interesting passages they themselves read in books are graphic accounts of scenes or events which they have witnessed themselves. The charm of all good description consists in its presenting to the reader, in spirited, graphic language, that with which he is most perfectly familiar. Hence it happens that if we take up a traveller's account of our country, we turn first to read the description which he has given of our own town; partly, perhaps, from curiosity to know his opinion of us, but still, in a great degree, for the simple pleasure of seeing through the medium of language that with which we are perfectly familiar by sight.

Our object then, in talking to children, is not to find something new, strange, and wonderful. We have only to clothe in language such conceptions and truths as they can understand, without racking our minds to produce continual novelty. Conversation conducted thus, though at first view might seem mere amusement, will in fact be very useful. The child will rapidly acquire familiarity with language by it, which is one of the most important acquisitions he can make. Then you will say a great deal which will be new to your child, though it may seem common place to you. Although you may not always aim at moral instruction, the narratives and descriptions you give will convey a moral expression which will have great influence upon him.

Parents occasionally express concern that there may be danger in narrating anything to children which is not historically true, lest it should lead them first to undervalue strict truth and finally to form the habit of falsehood. These fears are not without some grounds, for it does require careful watch and constant effort to form and preserve a habit of honesty in children. Whether you relate fictitious stories to them or not, you will often find in them propensities to deceit and falsehood, which it will sometimes require all your moral power to withstand. We cannot, therefore, avoid the danger of children falling into the sin of falsehood. The only question is, how we can most advantageously meet and overcome it.

Now it seems to me that we cannot accomplish this by confounding fictitious narration with falsehood, and condemning both. No one pretends that the narration of fictitious incidents is in itself criminal. The objection is that such fiction may have a tendency to lead to what is criminal; the intention to deceive being essential to the guilt of falsehood. The question is then where, in attempting to guard children from falsehood, we can most advantageously take our stand. Shall we assume the position that all narration which is not historically true is wrong? Or shall we show them that the intention to deceive is the essence of the guilt of falsehood, and contend only against that? My own opinion is that it is easier and better, in every respect, to do the latter. If you bring them at once to the line which divides honesty and deception, they can see easily and readily that you have brought them to the boundaries of guilt. In maintaining this distinction, you will have reason and conscience clearly assenting; consequently, you can raise the strongest fortification against sin. On the other hand, if you extend your lines of defense so as to include what you admit is not wrong, but only supposed to be dangerous, you extend greatly your circle of defense, you increase the difficulty of drawing a clear line of demarcation, and, notwithstanding all you can do or say, your theory condemns the mode of instruction adopted by the Savior Jesus Christ.

Therefore, we may indulge the imagination freely in children; but we must raise an impassable wall, on the first confines of intention to deceive, and guard it with the greatest vigilance.

For example, if a little child should ask for a story, perhaps you might say:

"Shall I tell you something real or something imaginary?"

"What is imaginary?"

"Suppose I make up a story about a squirrel who lived in the woods by the name of Chipperee, and tell you what he did all day; how he came out of his hole in the morning, what he saw, what he found to eat, and what other squirrels he met, and about his going down to a little brook to drink and carrying home nuts for the winter. If there never was any such squirrel and I made up the whole story, that would be imaginary."

"But father, that would not be true. Is it not wrong to say anything that is not true?"

"No, it is not always wrong to say what is not strictly true. If I were to say anything that was not true in order to deceive you, that would be wrong. For example, if I had some bitter medicine to give you and I covered it with sugar and told you it was all sweet sugar, that would be wrong. But if I imagine a story about a squirrel just to amuse you and teach you in a more pleasant way how squirrels live, and then if I tell you plainly that it is not a true account of any particular squirrel, would you think that there would be anything wrong in that?"

Thus it seems that in this case, as in most others, it would be easiest and safest, as well as most Biblical, to draw the line at the real point where guilt begins. Here only is there a tangible, moral distinction which children can appreciate, and though the work of keeping them off of the forbidden grounds of deception and falsehood will require, in any case, much effort and care, it seems as if this is the most proper place to stand. However, if after mature reflection, any parents think differently and still consider all fiction dangerous, they ought to be controlled by their own convictions and abstain from it altogether.

We have mentioned three great classes of subjects which may supply parents with means of conversation with their children, so as to gratify their almost insatiable appetite for knowledge. We have gone fully into this part of the subject, on account of the universality of the complaint on the part of those who have the care of young children, that they do not know what to tell them.

Having thus attempted to show those interested in children what to tell them, we may perhaps devote a few paragraphs to considering the best way to tell it.

Address the mind of the child through the senses; through those faculties of the mind by which the impressions of the senses are recognized or recalled. In other words, present everything in such a way that it may convey vivid pictures to the mind. In childhood, the senses are emphatically the great avenues to knowledge. I can best illustrate what I mean by contrasting two ways of telling the same story:

"A man had a fine dog and he was very fond of him. He used to take good care of him and give him all he wanted. In fact, he did all he could to make him comfortable so that he would enjoy a happy life. Thus, he loved his dog very much and took great pleasure in seeing him comfortable and happy."

This now presents very few sensible images to the mind of the child. In the following form, it would convey the same general ideas, but far more distinctly and vividly.

"There was once a man who had a large, black and white dog beautifully spotted. He made a little house for him out in a sunny corner of the yard, and used to give him as much meat as he wanted. He would go and see him sometimes, and pat his head while he was lying upon his straw in his little house. He loved his dog."

No one at all acquainted with children need be told how much stronger an interest the latter style of narration would excite.

The difference is that the former is expressed in abstract terms, which the mind comes to appreciate fully only after long habits of generalization, while in the latter, the meaning comes through sensible images which the child can picture to himself with ease and pleasure. This is the key to one of the great secrets of generating interest in children, and in teaching the young generally. Approach their minds through the senses. Describe everything as it presents itself to the eye and to the ear in great detail.

The intelligent reader will be able to apply this rule to all the classes of subjects in education. We might well follow out the principle, its illustration and application to the various stages of childhood and youth, and the proper limits of it, for its limits must be observed or else we shall make the pupil helplessly dependent upon his senses for life. There is, however, little danger of passing these limits in early years. The great difficulty with instructions and addresses to children, and the books written for them, is not lack of simplicity as is commonly supposed, but too much generality and abstractness.

This leads me to my final recommendation. Let your style be abrupt and striking, and give the reins entirely to the imagination. Aim at the utmost freedom of form and manner, and let your tones and inflections be highly varied. The tones expressive of emotion are instinctive, not acquired. This is proved by their universal similarity among all nations. The style, too, should be abrupt and pointed, and everything illustrated with action. At least, this is one element of interest that should be used in a greater or lesser degree at discretion.

We will consider one final example to illustrate this point. It is our story of the man who was kind to his dog. We have given two modes of commencing it, the second adding very much to the interest which the child would take in it. But by our present rule of giving abruptness and point, and striking transition to the style, we can give it a still greater power. Suppose the narrator, with a child on each knee, begins by saying:

"One pleasant morning a man was standing upon the steps of his door, and he said, 'I think I will go and see my dog Towser.' Now, where do you think his dog Towser lived?"

"I don't know," will be the reply of each listener with a face full of curiosity and interest.

"Why old Towser was out in a little square house which his master had made for him in a corner of the yard. So he took some meat in his hand for Towser's breakfast. Do you think he took out a plate, a knife, and fork? This man was very kind to Towser – his beautiful, spotted, black and white Towser – and when he got to his house he opened the door and said, 'Towser, come out here Towser.' So Towser came running out and stood there wagging his tail. His master patted him on the head. You may jump down on your hands and feet and I will tell you exactly how it was. You shall be Towser. Here, you may get under the table which will do for his house. Then I will come and call you out and pat you on the head."

We go into these minute details with no little hesitation, since some of our readers may perhaps consider them beneath the dignity of a book for adults. To know how to make a single child happy for half an hour is indeed a little thing, but the knowledge acquires importance and dignity when we consider how many millions of children there are to be affected by it; how many half hours in the life of each may be rescued from vain idleness and boredom by these means. Thus the objects, though comparatively trifling when regarded in detail, rise to dignity and importance when we consider their vast application.

This particular style, with varied modes of illustration mingled with action, will give spirit and interest even to many moral instructions. But we must not dwell on this point; we must pass on to the third great characteristic of childhood. The reader will, we hope, keep in mind the plan of our discussion. We are considering some of the great characteristics of childhood, preparatory to some practical directions for gaining through them an access to the heart. Having examined love of action and love of acquiring knowledge, we now pass to the third.

**To love those from whom they receive aid and sympathy in their desires.**

Gratitude in the young partakes of the general child-like qualities of their character, and it is not very surprising that it should be most strongly awakened by such kindness as they can most sensibly appreciate.

There are two conditions of affection on the part of children. First, the kindness intended should be on their level; it should show itself in favors which they can understand and appreciate.

This tendency in the heart of a child is in perfect keeping with the general laws of human nature, with respect to gratitude and love. These feelings are awakened, not by the deeds of kindness which we experience from others, but by the feelings of kindness of which we consider the deeds an indication. It is a sympathetic action of heart upon heart while actions, words, and looks, are the medium. Consequently, the effect is not in proportion to the greatness of the favors, but to the distinctness with which they move the mind of the receiver to the love which originated them. Hence it is, that unless the kindness you render to children is such as they can fully appreciate, it will not produce its proper effects. Many persons are often surprised to see how easily some of their acquaintances will gain the affection of children, and acquire an influence over them. But this is the secret of it. They come down to the child's level in the nature of the favors they show to them: they excite or employ their mental powers, they speak a kind word indicating interest in their play or pursuits, they aid them in their own little schemes, or they at least regard them with looks and words of kindness. These are indications of a feeling of kindness which the child can understand, and as we have seen before, it is in proportion to the distinctness with which the feeling of kindness is perceived in one's heart that gratitude and affection are awakened in another.

The second condition on which the affection and gratitude of children is to be secured is that the favors which call for it should be sincere, or at least that the child should have sufficient evidence of sincerity. A splendid toy, however adapted to interest the child, if sent to him by a relative or an acquaintance of his parents who really cares little about him, will be received with selfish gratification perhaps, but with little gratitude towards the donor. In fact, this condition stands on the same foundation with the other. The child must see through the favor bestowed a feeling of real kindness in the one who bestowed it, for it is this emotion in one's heart which, by a kind of sympathy, awakens the corresponding emotion in another. The present or the favor aids only as the medium by which the inter-communication is made. Thus one person may give the most valuable and costly presents to two children, while another will produce a stronger impression upon their hearts, awaken a more friendly feeling, and connect himself with them by more pleasant and permanent associations by the mere manner in which he talks with them while they are playing in the street.

**To catch the spirit and imitate the actions of those whom they love.**

Probably this imitative, or rather sympathetic principle has more influence in the formation of early character than any other. Associations and sympathy have far more influence with children than does argument or reasoning. How often do parents attempt to reason with children in respect to some duty or command to hasten the performance, when the result is directly the reverse? The discussion unsettles the subject and throws a doubt about the duty, for argument presupposes a question with respect to the subject of it. It, therefore, almost always makes it harder for the child to obey than it was before. Reasoning upon the general principles of duty when the mind of the pupil is in a calm state is highly important as a branch of instruction, as will hereafter show more fully. However, reasoning has comparatively little effect upon the formation of the habits and character. The cause of this is that the powers of associated logic are among the last that are developed, certainly among the last to come in for a share in the government of the conduct and character. If the reader has the disposition and the skill to experiment a little upon childhood in this respect, he will be astonished to find how feeble and unformed are the powers necessary for perceiving a logical sequence, and how entirely a pleasant association will usurp the place and exercise the control belonging legitimately to sound deduction. Hence the numerous prejudices and presuppositions of childhood, as for instance the preference for the small silver coin over the large bank note. Argument and explanation are often entirely insufficient to overcome the associations of value connected with the appearance of the former.

On a question of a name for an infant brother, a boy three or four years old expressed and persisted in a preference for George over Francis, which was generally voted for by the family. To see how great and unquestioned the control of mere association might be in his mind, I said to him, "If his name is Francis, you can, once he grows up, say, 'Mother, may I take Francis out for a ride?' And mother will say, 'Yes.' Then you can take Francis up, carry him out, and put him in your little wagon. Then you can take hold of the handle and say, 'Francis, are you all ready?' Francis will say 'Yes.' Then you can draw him about a little way, and after a while bring him back and say, 'Here, mother, I have brought Francis back safe.' Do you not think, then, that his name had better be Francis?"

"Yes, I do," he said cordially, convinced and converted completely by this precious specimen of logic.

Thus the reader will find, on scrutinizing the conduct of children, that pleasant associations have more influence in determining their preferences and habits — moral, intellectual, and physical — than almost all others. The reasoning powers ought to be cultivated, and to cultivate them successfully children must be led to employ them on the various subjects which daily come before them. However, while this process is going on we must take care that the other great avenue to the soul, which is opened so early and which affords so easy an access, is occupied well.

If then, in accordance with the previous heads of this discussion, you take such an interest in the children around you as to secure their gratitude and love, you will form in their minds strong, pleasant associations with your character, which hopefully is consistently Biblical. You will find, consequently, that you will have an immense influence over them. They will think as you think and feel as you feel. They will catch your expressions and the tone of your voice, your looks and your attitudes, your habits and your peculiarities — both good and bad. So he who associates freely with children, and by his sympathy and regard for them acquires their love, will leave an image of his own character upon theirs which years of future life will never remove.

Many parents stand aloof from their children, occupied by business and cares, or else have no sympathy with their peculiar feelings and childlike propensities. The heart of the father, therefore, does not keep so near to that of the child that there may be communicated to the one the healthy, virtuous action of the other. This place of influence is left to be taken possession of by anybody, a cousin, a neighbor, or a boy in the streets, and the father aims at forming the character of his son by lecturing to him from time to time as his occupations may give him opportunity, plenty of sound argument and good advice! The boy receives them in silence and the father hopes that they produce an impression. The downward progress which his heart is making by his intimacy with sin is not perceived, but at last, when he is twenty, it can be no longer concealed and the father perceives to his astonishment that all his good instructions have been utterly thrown away. It is the ascendancy of affection, and that founded on such evidences of interest and good will as the child can himself appreciate, which will alone give us any considerable power; and if we secure the affection we shall inevitably wield the power.

Having thus considered the first general division of this chapter according to our plan, we pass to the second.

### PRACTICAL DIRECTIONS

Make it a special object of attention and effort to gain an influence over the minds of the children whom you shall find within your reach. Parents often pay too little attention to this. Their fellowship with children is only the necessary contact of command and obedience. A father who devotes some time daily to involving himself in the pursuits and pleasures of his children: talking with them, playing with them, or reading stories to them, will gain an ascendancy over them which, as they grow up, will be found to be immensely powerful. They are bound together by common feelings, by ties of affection and companionship, which have a most controlling moral influence upon the heart. It is, however, often neglected.

The man overwhelmed with business or burdened with cares does not descend to the level of the child. He sees that his boys are trained up according to rule, confined by proper restraints, and supplied with proper instruction. However, no strong ties of interest or affection reconcile the little pupil to the restraints or give allurement to the instruction. Consequently, when he is passing from twelve to fifteen, or from fifteen to twenty, the parent gradually finds that though all has been right to his eye, his child's heart has been going on in a course totally different from the one he intended. The alarmed and disappointed parent tries to bring back his son, but he finds to his surprise and sorrow that he has no hold upon him. Though they have had breakfast, lunch, and dinner together for fifteen years, they have been, in fact, strangers to each other all the time. They have moved in different circles, have had different pleasures, different pains, different hopes, and different fears. The son could not ascend to the region occupied by the father, and the father would not descend to that of the son. Thus they have been physiologically divorced, and the father finds that he has no hold over the heart of his child only when it is too late to acquire it.

But perhaps you are not a parent. You are an older brother or sister, still under your father's roof. If now, you really wish to do good, your most important sphere of duty is that little circle of children who, next to their parents, look up to you. In this case, it should be your first concern to gain an ascendancy over their minds; an ascendancy based on their regard for your moral worth, and an affection inspired by your kindness and interest in them.

In the same manner, whatever may be your connection with children, whether you are their teacher in a Sunday school, their father or mother, their neighbor, or their brother or sister, you must first secure their interest and affection or you can do them little good. If they dislike you personally, they will instinctively repel the moral influence you may endeavor to exert upon them. If you have no sympathy with their childish feelings, you can gain no sympathy in their hearts for the sentiments and principles you may endeavor to inculcate upon them. If, however, you can secure their affection and sympathy, your power over them is almost unbounded. They will believe whatever you tell them and adopt the principles and feelings you express, simply because they are yours. They will catch the very tone of your voice and expression of your countenance, and spontaneously reflect the moral image, whatever it may be, which your character may hold up before them.

Never attempt to acquire an ascendancy over children by improper indulgence. It is one of the mysteries of human nature that indulgence never awakens gratitude of love in the heart of a child. The boy or girl who is most yielded to (most indulged), is always the most ungrateful, the most selfish, and the most utterly unconcerned about the happiness or the suffering of father and mother. Pursue a straight forward and firm course: calm, yet determined; kind, yet adhering inflexibly to what is right. This is the way to secure affection and respect, whether it be in the fellowship of parent with child, brother with sister, teacher with pupil, general with soldier, or magistrate with citizen. Yes, the youngest child, when allowed to conquer, though perhaps gratified at his success, has insight enough to despise the weakness and lack of principle which yielded to him. He cannot feel either respect or affection. In the same manner, you cannot depend upon presents. Unreasonable indulgence and profusion of presents are the two most common modes of endeavoring to buy the good will of the young. But, the slightest knowledge of human nature ought to teach us that love cannot be bought. Presents alone have far less influence in awakening the affection and gratitude of children than do kind words. The most valuable gift, coldly given, will not win a boy's heart half as much as sitting down with him for a few minutes on the carpet to help him make his little log cabin.

Once the ascendancy and the influence thus described is gained over the children with whom you are connected, the rest of the work is easy. You have only to exhibit right conduct, and exemplify and express right feelings, and they will spontaneously imitate the one and insensibly, but surely, follow the other. This they will inevitably do, whether the expectation of it be a part of your plan or not. Whatever principles they see that you habitually cherish, they will themselves adopt. If you are fond of dress, applause, admiration, or money, the children who hear your conversation, if they love you, will learn to be fond of them, too. If they see that you love duty and your Savior, and if you are living in the habitual fear of sin and in steady efforts to prepare for a future world, they will feel a stronger influence leading them to the same choice than any other human means can exert. In a word, if they love you, there will be a very strong tendency in their hearts to vibrate in unison with yours.

But this simple possession of the right feelings and principles is not enough. That is, though it will alone accomplish a great deal, it will not alone affect all that may be effected. You must distinctly express good sentiments in their hearing, as well as exemplify them in your conduct. In the school room, on the Sabbath, by the fireside, and in your walks, take occasion to express what is right. I do not mean here to prove it, explain it, or illustrate it; I mean to express it. Clothe it in language. Give truth utterance. There is more in this than mankind generally supposes. In many cases, when an argument on a moral subject is successfully presented to a popular audience, the logical force of the argument is not the secret of the effect. The work is done by the various statements of the proposition directly or indirectly contained in the train of reasoning, enunciations which produce their effect as simple expressions of the truth. There is something in man which enables him to seize by direct comprehension, what is true and right and proper, when it is distinctly presented to him. He sees its moral fitness by a sort of direct moral vision, he has an appetite for it, as for food, which is only to be presented in order to be received.

This is specially true of children, for in them the powers of reasoning are not developed, and consequently the susceptibility of being influenced by reasoning is smaller in proportion than with the mature.

For example, you are walking with a little child on a pleasant morning during the last days of February. As you walk on the crust of the snow, a little snow bird hops along before you and picks the seeds from the stems of the herbage which the wintry storms have not entirely covered. Now the most sound and intelligent argument you can offer the child in favor of kindness to animals would not have half as much power over him as some physical demonstration as this.

"Oh, see that little bird. Shall I throw my cane at him? Oh, no indeed! it would hurt him very much, or if it did not hit him it would at least frighten him very much. I am sure I would not hurt that little bird. He is picking up the seeds. I am glad he can find those little seeds. They taste very sweet to him, I suppose. I wish I had some crumbs of bread to give him. Do you think he is cold? No, he is all covered with warm feathers, so I do not think he is cold. Only his feet are not covered with feathers. I hope they are not cold."

Or if your companion is a boy of ten or twelve years of age, you may speak in a different manner while still you utter nothing but a simple expression of your kindness and interest, and by it you will awaken kindness and interest in him. You might say, "See that snow bird. Stop, do not let us frighten him. Poor little thing! I should think he would find it hard work living in these fields of snow. He is picking the seeds out of the tops of last year's plants. Let him have all he can find. There is a fine large weed by the side of that rock. I wish he could see it. We will move around this way and then perhaps he will hop towards the rock. There he goes. He has found it. Now stop and watch him feast himself."

On the other hand, suppose you say, "Stop, there's a snow bird. Stand back a minute and see how quickly I can knock him down with my cane. If I can hit him, I will make sure he will never hop again."

Now these are all mere expressions of your own feeling, and in nine cases out of ten the child who listens to them would find his heart gliding spontaneously into the same state with your own, whether it were that of kindness or of cruelty. This mere utterance of the sentiment or feeling of your heart would, except where some peculiar counteracting causes prevent it, awaken the like in him. Hence, be always ready not only to exhibit in your conduct the influence of right principle, but to express that principle in language. Many persons imagine that unless they explain, illustrate, or prove the truth, they can have nothing to say. But they err; it is the simple expression of it, pleasantly and clearly, in a thousand various ways and on a thousand different occasions, which will do more than either explanation, illustration, or proof.

But still, though the former is what produces comparatively the greatest effect, the latter must receive attention, too. Correct moral principle must not only be exhibited in your conduct and expressed in your conversation, it must also be formally illustrated and proved from time to time – this is of the utmost importance. The admission of moral principle to the minds of the young, and the formation of right habits of feeling, may perhaps be most easily received at first by means of these moral sympathies, but it is only in the calm and intelligent conviction of reason that Biblical morality can have any firm and lasting foundation for its throne. If your habitual conduct does not exhibit right principles, and your conversation express them, you can never bring your children to adopt them by any arguments for the truth. But if your habitual conduct and conversation is right, formal and logical instruction is necessary to permanently secure the conquests which these influences will certainly make.

One more practical direction remains. It does not arise very directly from the general views advanced in this chapter, and has in fact no special connection with them. It also relates more particularly to the duty of parents but it is so fundamentally important that it ought to be stated right here. It is, "keep children as much as possible by themselves, and away from evil influences." Keep them from bad company is very common advice. We may go much farther and say, keep them from the company of others unless their is a godly purpose for an assembly. Of course, this is to be understood with proper limits and restrictions, for to a certain extent associating with others is of high advantage to them, both intellectually and morally. But this extent is almost universally far exceeded, and it will be generally found that the most virtuous and the most intellectual are those who have been brought up with few companions. As an aside, it should be stressed that the most Biblical way for Christian parents to provide their children with quality socialization is for them to act upon the words of Psalm 127, and have large families!

In fact, a large portion of history and experience shows, and it is rather a dark sign in respect to sinful human nature, that the mutual influence of man upon man is an influence of deterioration and corruption. Where men congregate in masses there depravity thrives, and they can keep near to innocence only by being remote from one another. Thus densely populated cities are always most immoral: an army, a ship, a factory, a crowded prison, and great gangs of laborers working in common, always exhibit peculiar tendencies to vice. So with the young. Boys learn more evil than good from their playmates at school; a college student who is quiet and docile at home, is often wild, idle, and insubordinate during term time at college; and how often has a mother found that either one of two troublesome children seems subdued and obedient when the other is away. It seems as if human nature can be safe only in a state of segregation; in a mass it runs at once to corruption and ruin. The Tower of Babel and the trial of Jesus are but two examples that support the view that a congregation of men are prone to evil.

So then, as frequent interaction among the children of a town or a neighborhood is impeded, within proper limits and restrictions, the moral welfare of the whole will be advanced. Few companions and fewer intimacies, and many hours of solitary occupation and enjoyment, will lead to the development of the highest intellectual and moral traits of character. In fact, a youngster's resources may be considered as entirely unknown and unexplored if he cannot spend his best and happiest hours alone.

It is often said that the young must be exposed to the temptations and bad influences of the world in order to know what they are and to learn how to resist them. "They must be exposed to them," say these advocates of early temptation, "at some time or other, and they may as well begin in season in order to get mastery over them sooner." But this is not so. The exposure, if avoided in youth, is avoided principally forever. A virtuous man in any honest pursuit of life comes into very little contact or connection with vice. True, he sees and hears more or less of it every day, but his virtuous habits, associates, and principles are such that it is kept, as it were, at a sort of moral distance. It does not possess that power of contamination, which a corrupt school boy exercises over his comparatively innocent companion. A vast proportion of the vicious and immoral are made so before they reach adulthood, and accordingly, he who goes on safely through the years of his youth will generally go safely for the rest of the way.

The issue then, is not whether socialization is necessary for children to properly mature, since all children have social needs. Rather, the issue is whether parents should place a higher priority on the quality of socialization to which their children are exposed, instead of merely concerning themselves with the quantity of their children's social contacts.

Christian parents today are too often criticized for being selective and discerning when it comes to choosing which youngsters they will permit to interact with their children. Our nation's first President, George Washington, put the proper standard for socialization into clear focus when he wrote, "It is better to be alone than in bad company."

The principles which we have been inculcating in this chapter may then, in conclusion, be summed up thus: Children are eager to exercise continually their opening faculties, and to learn all they can about the world into which they are ushered. Those who aid and sympathize with them in these, their childlike feelings, they will love, and their principles and conduct they will adopt and imitate.

This being so, we have by rendering them this aid and sympathy, an easy way of gaining over them a powerful influence. Once this is gained, we must exemplify in our conduct, express in our daily conversation, and enforce by formal instructions, the principles which we wish them to grasp (and they will readily grasp them). Then to make our work sure, we must shelter their tender minds from those rude blasts of moral exposure which howl everywhere in this wilderness of sin. Any Christian who will act faithfully on these principles towards the children who are within his reach, will probably save many of them from vice and misery, and he will certainly elevate the temporal virtue and happiness of them all. And if he acts in these duties as the humble but devoted follower of Jesus Christ – sincere, unaffected, honest, and childlike himself – there are no labors in which he can engage for which he may, with greater confidence, invoke the intervention of the Holy Spirit, to bless them to the salvation of souls.

It is entirely likely that some adults will be tempted to take the instruction of this chapter lightly, to the extent that they will fail to exercise a consistently high standard of morality before children. Any individual so tempted is encouraged to remember the sobering words of the Lord Jesus Christ as he warned the crowds who assembled at his feet regarding the judgment reserved for those who influence children in an evil manner:

> *And whoso shall receive one such little child in my name receiveth me. But whoso shall offend one of these little ones which believe in me, it were better for him that a millstone were hanged about his neck, and that he were drowned in the depth of the sea. Matthew 18:5-6*

# Chapter 2

## How to Disciple a Young Person
## (The Story of Alonzo)

Modern child psychologists often tell us that the way to make a child happy is by teaching him how to love himself. The topic of sin is no longer beneficial to stress to a child according to psychologists; only "positive" words should be used to build self-esteem.

It is interesting to note that the Bible never once commands any human being to love himself. On the contrary, the Bible directs us to love God and our neighbor. (Any student of the Bible should already know that the major problem with fallen man is his tendency to love himself too much.)

The real gospel of Christ talks in terms of surrendering ourselves to Jesus. Contrary to this truth stands the self-love crowd who is seeking to encourage our nation's youth to "think more highly of yourselves than you ought to think."

Adults in America today who have a burden for the souls of children must rally around the old rugged cross and point children in the direction of the Savior who bled and died for their sins! The greatest blessing anyone can give to a child is to lead him to a knowledge of the Savior Jesus Christ, and to His love.

The story that follows gives any interested adult a thorough understanding of the inner workings of a child's heart, its deceptions and corruptions, and its greatest need, which is to be freed from the guilt and burden of sin. The primary purpose of the story is to clarify that the greatest need of a child's heart is to secure loving fellowship with Jesus Christ. It is not love of self that will satisfy the great longings of a child's heart. A child becomes truly happy when he is brought to the place where he can see that the love of Christ is the only foundation for real peace and joy.

Alonzo was a young boy who lived in Vermont. His father owned a farm in one of those warm and verdant dells which gave a charm to the scenery of the Green Mountains. The low, broad farmhouse, with its barns and sheds, hay stacks and high woodpiles, made almost a little village as they lay spread out in a sunny opening near the head of the glen. A winding road repeatedly crossing a brook, which meandered among the trees down through the valley, guided the traveller to the spot.

The wide yard was filled with domestic animals and the sheds were stored with utensils of the farm. Lilac trees and rose bushes ornamented the front of the dwelling, and from the midst of a little green lawn on one side of the house a deep clear spring, walled in with moss covered stones, poured up continually from below a full supply of cool, clear water. A group of willows hung over the spring and a well-trod foot path led to it from the house. A smooth flat stone lay before the "end door," as they called it, which led to the spring.

Here, during the second year of his life, Alonzo might have been seen almost every sunny day, playing with buttercups and daisies, or digging with his little shovel in the earth before the door, or building houses out of corn cobs taken from the granary. The next summer, had you watched him, you might have observed that his range was wider and his plans of amusement a little more enlarged. He had a garden, two feet square, where he stuck down green twigs broken from the shrubs around him; he would make stakes with a dull house knife partly for the pleasure of making them, and partly for the pleasure of driving them into the ground. He would ramble up and down the path a little way, and sometimes go with his mother down to the spring to see her dip the bright tin pail into the water and to gaze with astonishment at the effect of the commotion. The stony wall of the spring seemed always to be broken to pieces; its fragments waved and floated about in confusion until they gradually returned to their places of rest. This extraordinary phenomenon astonished him again and again.

One day Alonzo's mother saw him going alone towards the spring. He had grabbed his pail and was going to try the wonderful experiment himself. His mother called him back and instructed him to never go there alone. "If you go there alone," she said, "you will fall in and be drowned."

Alonzo was not convinced by the reason, but he was awed by

the command, and for many days he obeyed. At length, however, when his mother was occupied in another part of the house, he stole away softly down the path a little way.

There was a sort of a struggle going on within him while he was doing this. "Alonzo," said Conscience, for even at this early age Conscience had begun to be developed, "Alonzo, this is very wrong."

Conscience must be conquered, if conquered at all, not by direct opposition but by evasion and deceit, and the deceiving and deceitful tendencies of the heart are very early developed.

"I am not going down to the spring," said Alonzo to himself. "I am only going down the path a little way."

"Alonzo," said Conscience, again, "this is wrong."

"Mother will not see me, and I shall not go quite down to the water, so that no harm will be done," said the child to himself in reply, and went hesitatingly on.

"Alonzo," said Conscience a third time, but with a feebler voice, "you should not go any further."

"My mother is too strict with me; there can be no harm in my walking as far as this."

He lingered a little while about halfway down the path, then slowly returned, the dialogue between Conscience and his heart going on all the time. The latter had succeeded so well in its artful policy that when he came back he hardly knew whether he had done wrong or not. It did not seem quite right, and there was a sort of gnawing uneasiness within him, but his heart had succeeded by its evasions in making so much of a question of the whole transaction that he could not really say that it was clearly wrong. Alonzo had been taught that God had made him, and that He watched over him at all times, but some how or other he did not happen to think of Him at all during this affair. He had also understood something of his obligations to his mother, for her kindness and love to him; but he did not happen to think of her now in this light. The contest consisted simply, on one side, of the low murmurings of Conscience telling him sternly that he was wrong; and on the other, the turnings and shiftings of a deceitful heart trying to quiet, or at least to drown, her disruptive influences.

I have focused particularly upon the philosophy of this early sin, because this was the way in which Alonzo committed all his sins for many years afterwards. Conscience made him uncomfortable while he was transgressing, but his heart kept up such a variety of evasions and queries that whenever he was doing anything wrong, he never seemed to have a distinct idea that it was clearly and positively wrong. For instance, a few days after the transaction described above, his mother had gone away from home to run an errand. His sister, who had the care of him, had left him alone at the door. He took up the pail and began to walk slowly down the path. Conscience, defeated before and familiarized to a certain degree with transgression, allowed him to go without opposition for part of the way, but when she perceived that he was actually approaching the spring, she shook her head and renewed her low, solemn murmuring.

"Alonzo, Alonzo, you must not go there."

"I know I shall not fall in," said Alonzo to himself.

"Alonzo, " said Conscience again, "you must not disobey."

Alonzo tried not to hear her, and instead of answering, he said to himself, "It was many days ago that she told me not to go. She did not mean never."

This was true, yet it may seem surprising that Alonzo could for one instant deceive himself with such an argument. But anything will do to deceive ourselves when we are in the mood. When we are committing sin we love to be deceived about it. Hence, it is very easy for a corrupted heart to justify wrong.

While saying that his mother could not have meant that he must never go, Alonzo leaned over the spring and tremblingly plunged in his pail. The special effect was produced. The stones and moss waved and quivered, to Alonzo's inexpressible delight. His mind was in a state of feverish excitement: Conscience calling upon him, in vain trying to make him hear; Fear whispering eagerly, that he might be seen; Curiosity urging him again and again to repeat his wonderful experiment.

Alonzo was a very little child, and the language in which I am obliged to clothe his thoughts and words correctly describes the thoughts and feelings which really passed within his bosom.

At length, he hastily drew out his pail and went back to the house. Conscience endeavored, when the excitement of the experiment was over, to gain his attention. Nevertheless, his heart was still bent on deceiving and being deceived.

"My mother said," thought he, "that I should fall in and be drowned if I went there, and I did not fall in. I knew I would not fall in."

Thus, instead of thinking of his guilt and disobedience, he was occupied with the thought of the advantage he had gained over his mother; that is, the heart which ought to have been penitent and humbled under the burden of sin was deluding itself with the false colors which it had spread over its guilt, being filled with deceit and self-congratulation.

Year after year passed on, and Alonzo grew in strength and stature; but he continued about the same in heart. Instead of playing on the round, flat door stone, he at length might be seen riding on his father's plough, or tossing about the drying grass in the mowing field, or gathering berries upon the hill side, on some summer afternoon. He was continually committing sins in the manner already described. These sins were different in circumstance and character as he grew older, but their nature, so far as the feelings of the heart were concerned, were the same. There was the same murmuring of Conscience, the same windings and evasions of his heart, the same self-deception, and the same success in leading himself to doubt, whether the act of transgression which he was committing, was right or wrong. His parents in most respects brought him up well. They taught him his duty, and when they knew that he did wrong, they disciplined him seriously, or if necessary, they punished him. Thus his conscience was cherished and he was often deterred by her voice from committing many sins. She held him regularly in check. His parents formed in him many good habits which he adhered to faithfully as habits, and thus so far as the influence of his parents could go he was, in most cases, deterred from the commission of sin.

Other things, equally sinful, he did without scruple. For example, he would have shuddered at stealing even a pin from his sister, but he would by unreasonable wishes and demands give her as much trouble, and occasion her as much loss of enjoyment, as if he had stolen a very valuable article from her. If he had undertaken to steal a little picture from her desk, Conscience would have thundered so terribly that he could not possibly have proceeded, but he could tease and vex her by his unreasonable and selfish conduct without any regret. If his heart had been honest and shrewd in discovering its own real character, these cases would have taught him that his honesty was artificial and accidental, and did not rest on any true foundation. But his heart was neither honest nor shrewd in respect to itself; it loved to be deceived. When he read of a theft in a good story book, he took great pleasure in thinking what a good honest boy he was in comparison.

He would not have forgotten to say his prayers, both morning and night. But, whenever he committed sin during the course of the day, he never thought of going away alone before God to confess it and to ask forgiveness. If his heart had been honest and shrewd in discovering his own character, this would have taught him that his piety was all a mere form, and that he had no real affection for God. His heart, however, was not honest, and though he never thought much about it, he still had an impression on his mind that he was the friend of God and that he regularly worshiped Him. He knew very well that he sometimes committed sin, but he did not suppose that it was often. He often succeeded in blinding or misleading Conscience to make it doubtful. If he could succeed in making a question of it, he would go and commit the sin, with a half-formed idea of examining the case afterwards. But then when the pleasure of the sin was over, he found the true moral character of the transaction to be rather a disagreeable subject to investigate; so he left it in his memory to fester and rankle there. Though he had such a number of these recollections as to give him no little uneasiness and annoyance, he still thought he was a very virtuous and promising young man.

When he was about twelve years old, Alonzo made a discovery which startled and alarmed him. Some young men had formed a plan of ascending a certain mountain summit which projected like a spur from the main range, and which reared its rocky head among the clouds, in full view of his father's farm. They had fixed upon Sunday evening for this purpose, an hour or two before sundown. "A great many people," said one of the boys, "think that the Sabbath ends at sunset, and an hour or so before will not make any great difference. We must climb up in time to see the sun go down." This disposal of the difficulty was abundantly satisfactory to all those who were inclined to go, but Alonzo had some doubts whether it would appear equally conclusive to his father and mother. One thing favored, however: his father was away, having been absent on some business for the town for several days. Alonzo thought that there was at least a possibility that his mother would find the deficiencies in the reasoning made up by a little extra persuasion, and that her consent to his sharing in the pleasure of the excursion would be obtained. At any rate, it was plainly worthwhile to try.

He came in on Saturday afternoon, and standing by the side of his mother, who was finishing some sewing necessary to complete her preparations for the Sabbath, nervously presented his request. She listened to him with surprise, and then told him he must not go.

"It would be very wrong," she said.

"But mother, we shall walk along very still. We will not laugh or play. It will only be taking a little walk after sundown."

Alonzo's mother was silent.

"Come, mother," said the boy, hoping that he had made some impression, "do let me go. Do say yes, just this once."

After a moment's pause, she replied:

"Some persons do indeed suppose that the Sabbath ends at sundown, but we think it continues until midnight, and we cannot shift and change the hours to suit our pleasures. Now, with all your resolutions about walking quietly, you know very well that such an expedition, with such companions, will not be keeping holy the Sabbath day. You therefore come to me with a proposal that I will allow you to disobey, directly and openly, one of the plainest of God's commands. It is impossible that I should consent."

While his mother was saying these words, emotions of anger and indignation began to rise and swell in Alonzo's bosom. Foreseeing how the sentence would end, he began to walk off towards the door and, just before the last words were uttered, he was gone. He shut the door violently, muttering to himself, "It is always just so."

In a state of wretchedness and sin (which my readers must conceive of if they have ever acted as Alonzo did), he walked out of the house and sank down upon a bench which he had made in the little orchard. Here he gave full flow for a few minutes to the torrent of boiling passion which had so suddenly burst out of his heart. In a short time, however, the excitement of his feelings subsided a little, and there came suddenly a sort of flash of moral light which seemed to reveal to him for an instant the true character of the transaction.

Something within him seemed to say, "What an unreasonable, ungrateful, wicked boy you are, Alonzo. Here is your mother, as kind a mother as ever lived. You owe her your very being. She has taken care of you for years, without any return, and has done everything to make you happy; and now, because she cannot consent to let you do what is most clearly wrong, your heart is full of anger, malice, and revenge. What a heart! Love and duty are forgotten, and every feeling of gratitude for long years of kindness is obliterated by one single interference with your wicked desires."

This reflection occupied but an instant in passing through Alonzo's mind. It flashed upon him for a moment, and was gone. The dark, heavy clouds of anger rolled over his soul again. He sat upon the bench in moody silence.

After several minutes, he again began to see that he was very wrong; such feelings towards his mother were, he knew, unreasonable and sinful, and he determined that he would not indulge them. So he rose and walked through a small gate into the yard where a large pile of long logs were lying, one of which had been rolled down and partly cut off. He took up the axe and went to work. But he soon learned that it was one thing to see that his feelings were wrong, and another thing to feel right. His mind was in a sort of chaos. Floating visions of the party ascending the hill, vexation at his disappointment, uneasiness at the recollection of his unkind treatment of his mother, all mingled together in his soul. "I wish I could feel right towards mother about this," he said to himself; but somehow or other, there seemed gathering over his heart a kind of dogged sullenness which he could not break or dispel. He concluded it was best to forget the whole affair for the present. So, he laid down the axe and began to pick up some chips and sticks to carry in for kindling the morning fire. He secretly determined that when he went in and met his mother again he would not show his impatience and anger, but would act "just as if nothing had happened."

Just as if nothing had happened! How, after such an act of disrespect, ingratitude, and disobedience, could he act as if nothing had happened! One would think that Alonzo would have great trouble with this self-centered plan.

But Alonzo did not make any such reflection. His heart clung to his sin and loved to be deceived by it. It seemed to him impossible to feel the relenting of true, heartfelt penitence, the love and gratitude which he knew his mother deserved, and especially that cheerful acquiescence in her decision which he knew he ought to feel. So he concluded to forget all about it. The poisoned fountain which had so suddenly burst forth in his heart was covered up again, smoothed over, yet ready to boil out anew upon any new occasion.

This and a few other similar occurrences led Alonzo to think that there might be deeper sources of moral difficulty in his heart than he had been accustomed to imagine, but he did not think much about it. His life passed on without much thought or regard for his character or his prospects as a moral being. He had, however, a sort of standing suspicion that there was something wrong, but he did not stop to examine the case. The little uneasiness which this suspicion caused was soothed and quieted a good deal by a sort of prevailing idea: that there was a great deal that was very excellent in his conduct and character. He was generally considered a good boy. He knew this very well, and one of the grossest of the forms of deceitfulness which the heart assumes is to believe that we deserve all that others give us credit for, even where the good qualities in question are merely the most superficial and shallow pretense. There is no manner of deceit quite so destructive to one's moral excellence as self-deceit.

An incident occurred about this time which almost opened Alonzo's eyes to the true character of some of his virtues. During the winter months he went to school, and the good qualities which he fancied he exhibited there were among those on which he most prided himself. One afternoon, as he was walking home with a green satchel full of books slung over his shoulder, he stopped a few minutes at the brook which crossed the road and looked down over the bridge upon the smooth dark colored ice which covered the deep water. It looked so clear and beautiful; he went down and cautiously stepped upon it. It was so transparent that it seemed impossible that it could be strong. He sat down on a stone which projected out of the water, and while he was there his teacher came along, and stopping on the bridge he began to talk with him. Alonzo and the teacher were on very good terms, and after talking together a few minutes at the brook they both walked along together.

Their way was a cross path through the woods, which led by a shorter course than the main road, to the part of the town where they were both going.

As they were stepping over a low place in the log fence where their path diverged from the road the teacher said, "Alonzo, I am glad to see you carrying your books home."

"I like to study my lessons at home in the evenings," said Alonzo with a feeling of secret satisfaction.

"Well, Alonzo, what would you say if I should tell you I could guess exactly what books you have in your satchel?"

"I don't know," Alonzo replied, "perhaps you saw me put them in."

"No, I did not."

"Well, you can tell by the shape of the books which you can see by looking at the satchel."

"No," said the teacher, "I see you have either your writing book or your Atlas, but I could not tell which by the appearance of the satchel. I see that there is by the side of it one middle sized book, too, but merely its size will not tell whether it is your Arithmetic, your Geography, or your Grammar."

"Well, what do you think they are?"

"I think they are your writing book and your spelling book."

There was in Alonzo's countenance an appearance of surprise and curiosity. He said the teacher was right, and asked him how he knew.

"I know by your character."

"By my character!" said Alonzo, "What do you mean by that?"

"I will tell you, though I think it will give you pain rather than pleasure. You are one of the best boys in my school, you give me very little trouble, and you are generally diligent in your duties – obedient and faithful. Now, have you ever thought what your motives are for this?"

"No sir, I have never thought about them particularly. I want to improve my time and learn as much as I can, so as to be useful when I am a man."

Alonzo thought that ought to be his motive, and so he fancied that it was. He did not mean to tell a falsehood. He did not say it because he wished to deceive his teacher, but because his heart had deceived him. It is so with us all.

"You think so, I have no doubt. But now I wish to ask you one question. What two studies do you think you are most perfect in?"

Alonzo did not like to answer, though he knew that he prided himself much on his handsome writing and on his being almost always at the head of his class in spelling. At length he said, with a modest air, that he thought he "took as much interest in his writing and in his spelling lessons, as in anything."

"Are there any studies that you are less advanced in than these?"

"Yes, sir."

"Well," said the teacher, "now I want to ask you another question. How is it that the writing book and the spelling book, which represent the two studies in which you have made the greatest proficiency, and in which you, of course, least need any extra efforts, are the very ones which you are bringing home to work on in the evenings?"

Alonzo did not answer immediately. In fact, he had no answer at hand. He thought that if he was inclined to study out of school hours, he had a right to take any books home that he pleased; however, he did not say so.

"And I should like to ask you one more question," said the teacher. "In what study do you think you are most deficient?"

"I suppose it is my Arithmetic," replied Alonzo, recollecting how he disliked, and avoided as much as possible, everything connected with calculation.

"And do you ever carry home your Arithmetic to study in the evening?"

Alonzo shook his head.

"Now you know that there are few subjects more important to a man than a knowledge of figures. How does it happen then, if your motive is to fit yourself for usefulness and happiness when a man, that the very study in which you are most deficient is the very one in which you never make any voluntary effort?"

There was a little pause, during which Alonzo looked serious. He felt very unhappy. It seemed to him that his teacher was unkind. He was purposely bringing his books home to study his lessons for the next day in order to please the teacher, and to be blamed just because he had not planned to bring his arithmetic instead of his spelling was very hard. Tears came to his eyes, but he strove to suppress them and said nothing.

"I know, Alonzo," continued the teacher, "that these questions of mine shall trouble you. I have not, however, asked them for the sake of troubling you, but for the purpose of letting you see into your heart and learn a lesson of its deceitfulness. I want you to think of this tonight when you are alone, and perhaps I will some day talk with you again."

So saying, they came out into the road again near the teacher's residence. They bid one another goodbye, and Alonzo walked on alone.

"He means," thought Alonzo, "that if I honestly wanted to improve, I should take greater interest in the studies in which I am deficient." As this thought floated through his mind it brought after it a dim, momentary vision of the pride, vanity, and love of praise which he suddenly saw revealed as the secret spring of all those excellences at school on which he had prided himself. But seeing all those fancied virtues of industry, love of learning, and desire to be conscientious and faithful, wither at once under the influence of two simple questions and turn into vanity, afforded him no pleasant subject of reflection. He was, therefore, glad to see a load of wood coming into his father's yard as he approached it, and he hastened to help him unload it. He thus got rid of the disagreeable subject without actually deciding whether the teacher was right or wrong.

The affair, however, shook and weakened his faith in the good traits of his character. He did not come to the distinct conclusion that they were all hollow and superficial, but he had a sort of vague fear that they might prove so. This was another sort of uneasiness laid up in his heart, a part of the burden of sin which he bore without thinking much of it.

Thus Alonzo lived. From twelve he passed on to fifteen, and from fifteen to twenty. He became a strong, athletic young man, known and esteemed for his industry, frugality, and steadiness of character. The time drew near which was to terminate his minority, and at this age his moral condition might be summed up thus:

First, the external excellences of his character arose from the influence of his excellent education. This would have been no disparagement to Alonzo if they had been of the right kind. However, they resulted only from the restraints imposed by the opinions of those around him, from the influence of his conscience which had been cultivated by his parents, and ultimately from the discomfort which occurred when he acted directly counter to the power of habit. His industry, for instance, was based upon the last, his regard for the Sabbath upon the second, and his temperance and steadiness mainly upon the positive influence of others.

Second, he made no regular systematic effort to improve his character. In fact, he felt little interest in any plan of this kind. He was quite interested in the various plans of cultivation and improvement on his father's farm, but his heart was chiefly set upon the amusements with which the young people of the neighborhood had involved themselves in the hours when work was done: the sleigh ride, the singing school, the fishing party, and the hiking. In the evening he was occupied with some one of these enjoyments, and the next day at his work he was busy planning the next – thus life glided on. I do not mean that he was entirely careless about his character and prospects as a moral being; he did sometimes feel a little uneasiness about them. Such discoveries as I have already described gave him an occasional glimpse of the secrets of his heart. As to his character, he knew it was superficially fair. He prided himself a good deal upon the appearance it presented towards others, and he did not see how he could improve it much without making a thorough work among the motives and feelings of the heart. This he could not but strongly shrink from, so he passed quietly along and thought about other things.

Finally, there was no connection between his soul and God. I mean no spiritual connection, no communion, no interchange of thought or feeling. He was taught to repeat a prayer morning and evening, and this practice he continued, considering it one of his duties. As he grew up from boyhood, however, he often neglected it in the morning, until at length he omitted it then altogether; and he gradually found an increasing reluctance to say it at night. He often omitted it, not intentionally, exactly – he forgot it; or, he was very tired and went immediately to sleep. These omissions, however (which, by the way, were far more frequent than he imagined), did not trouble him as much as it might have been expected that they would, for he began to think that the practice was intended for children and that he was getting too mature for such things. When he did remember this duty, it was only a form. There was no communion or connection between him and God. So far as the feelings of his heart were concerned, he lived in independence of his Maker. God was irrelevant.

Such was Alonzo's condition during the winter before he was to be twenty-one. One evening during that winter a meeting was appointed at a local schoolhouse. A stranger was to preach. On such occasions the schoolhouse was always filled. The congregation came from the farmers' families for several miles around: curiosity regarding the stranger, the pleasure of a winter evening's expedition, the light from the great blazing wood fire beaming upon a hundred bright and cheerful countenances, and in at least some cases, an honest desire to know and do duty, constituted the motives which drew the assembly together. At six o'clock, Alonzo harnessed a strong, fleet, well-fed horse onto a colorfully painted sleigh, helped his father and mother into the back seat, and mounted himself upon a higher one in front; away they went jingling down the valley. They were lost to sight by the turnings of the road among the trees, and the sleigh-bells, sounding fainter and fainter, soon died away upon the ear.

A little before nine, Alonzo might have been seen returning slowly up the valley. The moon had risen and it shone through the trees, casting a beautiful white light upon the snowy wreaths which hung upon them. The horse walked along slowly, and Alonzo was making crosses with his whip-lash upon the smooth surface of the snow which bordered the road. He was lost in thought. The subject of the sermon was the importance of preparation for another world; and it happened, from some cause or other, that Alonzo's mind was in such a calm, contemplative state that evening that the discourse made a strong impression. It was not an impression made by any extraordinary eloquence. The preacher, in a quiet, simple manner presented truths which Alonzo had heard numerous times before, though heretofore they had, as it were, stopped at the ear. This night, they seemed to penetrate to his heart. He came out of the meeting thoughtful. He rode home silently. There seemed to be a new view opened before his mind. The future world appeared a reality to him; it looked near, and he wondered why he was not making a preparation for it. His father and mother rode in silence, too, each unconscious of the thoughts of the other but both thinking of their son. A rare and divine influence was moving upon the hearts of all.

These serious thoughts passed away the next day, but they left behind a more distinct impression than he had been accustomed to feel: that he had a great work to do before he left the world, and that was a work which he had not yet begun.

He was careful to say the prayer of his childhood that night, with great seriousness, and he made a great effort to think about what it meant while he was repeating it. It is true that there is a great, and one would suppose, sufficiently obvious distinction between having the meaning of a prayer in the mind, and having the feelings and desires it expresses in the heart. But Alonzo did not perceive this distinction. He thought very distinctly of the meaning of the several successive petitions and confessions, and that was all; but it was enough to satisfy a deceiving and deceitful heart, and Alonzo dismissed his cares on the subject of his preparation for death as he went to sleep, feeling that he had made a good beginning.

Alonzo's attention was occupied early the next morning by an excursion into the forest for a load of wood with his father, and he entirely forgot his new religious resolutions until the evening. This discouraged him a little. However, he again offered his prayer with an effort to keep its meaning in his mind, though that effort was less successful than on the evening before. His thoughts would slip away from his control, and while he was saying, "my sins have been numerous and aggravated," or "lead me not into temptation," he would find that his mind was dwelling upon the past scenes of the day; it would be off in the forest where he had been at work or surveying the smooth slopes of hay in the barn loft or dwelling with pleasure upon his favorite horse feeding in the stall.

Alonzo was so dissatisfied with his prayer that he began again before he got through, though with not much better success than before. He was upset with himself that he could not confine his attention more easily. He could not understand the nature of his problem. The obvious explanation was a heart alienated from God and governed by its own spontaneous tendencies. Willingly deceived, he was spiritually blind.

However, Alonzo's deceitful heart had succeeded so well that he thought his second prayer would do, and he gradually fell asleep.

Weeks passed on, and Alonzo made feeble efforts to be a religious man. He said nothing of his feelings to anyone. In fact, he would not have anybody know that he had any intention of serving God. Whether it was because he was ashamed to be seen in the service of such a Master, or because he thought that his new feelings were of so high a degree of moral excellence that modesty required he should conceal them, we do not say. He was, at any rate, very careful to conceal them.

He made, naturally, little progress. Weeks and months passed away, and it seemed to him that he remained in the same place. The truth was that there was a current carrying him down which he did not perceive, but whose effects at distant intervals were very evident. He moved like the little water skipper whose motions he had often watched on his father's brook, who now and then makes a convulsive and momentary effort to ascend but who is borne continually backwards by a current steady and unceasing in its flow so that, notwithstanding his leaps, he drifts insensibly down towards the gulf behind him.

Alonzo was also like the skipper in other respects. He distinctly saw his own repeated efforts, but the slow, gentle, continual operation of the current was unperceived. His face was turned up the stream, too, where all was smooth and sunny and beautiful. He did not see the dark gulf that yawned behind.

In a word, Alonzo made but little progress. The work was all uphill. He perceived that on the whole he was not advancing, and yet he could scarcely tell why. There were several difficulties, the operation of which he felt, but there was something mysterious and unaccountable about them.

First, he was continually forgetting all his good intentions. He would, for example, reflect sometimes on the Sabbath – upon his duties and obligations, and would resolve to be watchful all the coming week to guard against sin and to keep his heart right. But he found it very hard to control the conduct of one day by the resolutions of the preceding. Saturday night would come and he would wake up, as it were, from his dream of business and pleasure and find that his spiritual work had been entirely neglected and forgotten during the week. Half ashamed, and half vexed with himself, he would renew good resolutions to be again neglected and forgotten as before. What could he do? There was no lack of good intention in his hours of solitude, but how to give these intentions an arm long enough to reach through the week; how to make the resolutions of retirement binding upon the conduct during the business and bustle of life was a great frustration to him. If he did not think of his resolutions at the right time, of course he could not keep them, and he was unable to discipline his soul so it would think of them at the right time.

There was another difficulty which very much perplexed and troubled Alonzo in his attempts to reform himself. Sometimes it seemed impossible for him to control his wrong feelings. When he became upset and irritated, as he sometimes did about his work, or when out of humor on account of some restraint which his mother laid upon him, he was conscious that his feelings were wrong and he would struggle against them with all his strength, but he could not conquer them. He thought he succeeded partially, but he was deceived. It was even worse than he supposed. For all the effect of his struggling was only to restrain the outward manifestation of his feelings; they still burned on in his heart. They were too strong for him, he perceived; and then in his despondency he would get lost in the metaphysical difficulties of the question: namely, how far he could be blamed for what it seemed to him he could not help.

Thus, in ordinary temptations Alonzo never could think of his resolutions, and in extraordinary ones he never could keep them. He knew not what to do, yet he was not very anxious about it. There was indeed a vague idea floating in his mind that there was a great work to be done, a work which he was yet only partially performing. He determined to take hold of it in earnest soon. The winter was so cold that he could not conveniently spend as much time alone as he wished. He thought that when the warm spring evenings came he could enjoy more solitude; spring, therefore, would be a more convenient season. When spring came they were pressed with work, and Alonzo looked forward for a time of a little greater leisure. But when planting was done there was haying, and after haying, harvesting. Then Alonzo thought that in a few months he should be free, and that he would make such arrangements as to have the more perfect command of his own time. Thus he passed on, thinking that he was watching for an opportunity to do his duty. But he was deceived. The secret was an innate dislike and repugnance for the work of repentance.

There was a strange inconsistency in his ideas. When he tried to purify and reform his heart, he found that he could not do it. Still, he had an impression, vague and undefined yet fixed and confided in, that he could perform the task easily at any time; therefore it was of little consequence that he waited for a more convenient season.

This postponement of a thorough attention to the work did not give him any particular uneasiness, for he was conscious that though he was not doing his duty quite in earnest enough, he still was not entirely neglecting it.

Alonzo's father had purchased for him a small farm a mile or two from his own. For some months, Alonzo had been very interested in his preparations for taking possession of it when he turned twenty-one; then, for many months afterwards, his whole soul was engrossed in his plans and labors for repairing the premises, getting his stock in good order, and putting the first seed into the ground. During these months he remained a member of his father's family, his own little farmhouse being empty and desolate. Occasionally, however, a piece of furniture was brought there and he would carry it in and fix it in its place, and then survey it again with a look of satisfaction. First came a stained birch bureau, then a half dozen chairs, then a bed; a few simple implements for the kitchen followed, and a load of wood was piled up in the yard. In a short time, the house began to look as if it was really intended to be occupied.

Finally, lights were seen one evening by the distant neighbors in both the rooms, for there were but two. Busy preparations were going forward, and at eight o'clock Alonzo drove up to his door in his own sleigh and handed out, first his sister, and then the bride, whom he had brought to share with him the responsibilities of his new home.

Alonzo led his horse away to the barn, took off the harness, and fastened him to his crib, previously filled to the top with hay. While doing this, he could not help thinking of his obligations to God for the circumstances of prosperity, and the prospects of happiness under which his life had been commenced. He thought he ought to be grateful. But this, as he afterwards found, was a different thing from actually being grateful. At any rate, he could not help thinking of his obligations to God, and this reminded him of the question whether he should begin the important exercise of evening family prayer that first night in his new home.

"It is your duty to do it," said Conscience.

"You will not do it properly. You will be embarrassed and perplexed; you cannot begin tonight," said Distrust.

"Still," said Conscience again, "it is your duty to do it."

"You had better wait a day or two until you get settled. It will be much easier, and more pleasant then," said a lying spirit of evasion and delay.

"It is your duty to do it tonight," murmured Conscience again.

Distracted by the discordant thoughts within him, Alonzo cut short their clamor by saying to himself that he could not begin that night, and hurried in; and the murmurs of conscience grew feebler, and soon died completely away.

Alonzo was not to blame for his double-mindedness; he was not to blame for shrinking from embarrassment, or for considering the duty before him a real trial. However, if he had actually been grateful to God for His goodness, instead of merely thinking that he ought to be so, he would have strived to fulfill this duty towards Him, even if it had been ten times as painful to perform.

Alonzo found it harder and harder to begin, the longer he postponed it. A month passed away, and the duty continued to be neglected. It was his design to read the Bible every day, but it seemed rather awkward to sit down before his wife and read it silently and alone, so he gradually neglected that. At night as he went to bed he usually offered a brief prayer, which was a sort of compromise to Conscience to induce him to let her rest in peace. He did not, however, feel happy in this mode of life. Uneasiness and anxiety rankled in his heart more and more. One evening, after hearing a plain and heartfelt sermon from his minister in the schoolhouse near his farm, he heard him announce with pleasure, what in New England is called an inquiry meeting, the next evening at his house. The design of such a meeting is to afford an opportunity for more plain and direct religious instruction to those who feel a personal interest in it, rather than the formal discourse offered to a large assembly.

Alonzo and his wife both resolved to go, and early in the

evening they took their seats with twenty others around their pastor's fireside. Such a meeting is one of great interest and solemnity. It is understood that all present feel a direct personal interest in respect to their own salvation, and they come together with a stillness and solemnity, which scarcely any other assembly exhibits.

The pastor sat by the side of the fire. First he read a hymn; it was not sung. Then he offered a short and simple prayer. He then addressed the little assembly much as follows:

"The most important question which you can ask about yourselves is, 'Am I the friend or the enemy of my Maker?' Now, there is probably not one here who really feels that he is his Maker's enemy, and yet, it is very possible that there is at least some here who are truly God's enemies.

"God justly requires us all to love Him; that is, to feel a personal affection for Him and to act under the influence of it. They who do not, He considers as not belonging to His spiritual family. They are His enemies. Not that they are employed directly and intentionally to oppose Him – they make perhaps no demonstrations of actual hostility – but in heart they dislike Him. To determine, therefore, whether we are the friends or the enemies of God, we must ascertain whether our secret hearts are in a state of love or of dislike towards Him.

"Perhaps some of you are saying to yourselves while I make these remarks, 'I am sure I love God in some degree, though I know I do not love Him as much as I should. I pray to Him, I try in some things to do my duty, I am (in some degree at least) grateful for his goodness, and I cannot perceive in myself any evidence of a feeling of dislike or hostility.'"

The pastor was right, at least in one instance, for these were exactly the thoughts which were passing through Alonzo's mind.

"Now, it is a difficult thing to tell," he continued, "what the state of our hearts is; or rather, it is a very common thing to be deceived about it. I will tell you how.

"First, we mistake approbation for love. We cannot help approving God's character. We cannot deny His excellence of justice, mercy, and holiness, any more than we can the directness of a straight line which we look upon. Approbation is the decision of the intellect or of the moral sense, which is entirely independent from the convictions of the heart. I once asked a young man whether he thought he loved God. 'O yes,' he said, 'I certainly think our Maker is worthy of all our praise and gratitude.' He was completely blind to the distinction, you see. He thought his Maker was worthy. Of course, he could not help thinking so. The question is not whether God is worthy of love and gratitude, but whether we really render these feelings in our hearts. Now, it is very possible that if you look honestly into your hearts, you will find that all your supposed love for God is only a cold, intellectual admission of the excellence of His character. This may exist without any personal feelings of affection towards Him.

"The second delusion is similar. We pray and we make an effort to confine our attention to our prayers, or as we term it, to think of what we are saying. This we mistake for really feeling the desires which we express. I do not doubt that many of you are in the habit of prayer, and that you often strive to confine your mind to what you are saying. Now you may do all this, without having in the heart any real desire for the forgiveness, the holiness, and the other blessings you seek. In fact, the very effort you make to confine your mind proves, or rather indicates very strongly, that the heart is somewhere else; for the mind goes easily where the heart is, and stays there with very little effort.

"There is another delusion, similar to the previous one; that is, thanking God without gratitude. We see that He is our benefactor and that He deserves our gratitude. We say this and feel satisfied with it, never reflecting that this is a very different thing from actually feeling gratitude.

"For instance, we may rise in the morning, look out upon the pleasant landscape before us, and think of our comfortable home, our friends, and all our means of happiness, which we are now to enjoy for another day. We feel a kind of complacency in them which, connected with our knowing that they come from God, we mistake for gratitude. We thus often think we are grateful, when the only feeling is a pleasant recognition of the good enjoyed. The difference is shown in this, that this latter feeling has no effect upon the conduct, whereas real gratitude will lead us to take pleasure in doing our Benefactor's will. Even a painful duty will become a pleasant one, for we always love to make a sacrifice for one who has been kind to us, if we are really grateful to him."

Alonzo here recollected the evening when he took possession of his new home, thinking that he was grateful to God for it, while yet "he could not" do that evening what he knew was God's will.

"In a word," continued the pastor, "we mistake the convictions of the understanding and the moral sense for the movements of the heart; whereas, the former may be all right, and the latter all wrong. I will tell you now some of the indications that a person dislikes God in his heart, even if his understanding is right in respect to His character and His favors:

"He dislikes God when his feelings do not go forth spontaneously and pleasantly towards Him. A parent once said to his child, 'Have you not sometimes felt, when thinking of some person whom you loved and who was away from you, as if your heart went out to that person; and then, it seemed as if the distance between you was lessened, though it was not in reality? On the other hand, when you think of a person whom you do not like, your heart draws back and shrinks coldly from him.' Now just tell me in which of these ways is your heart affected when you think of God."

Alonzo recollected how readily, when he was at work on the hill-side or in the distant forest, his thoughts and affections would roam away to his wife and his home, and hover there. He saw clearly that his heart never once sought God in this manner.

"Another evidence of our disliking God is when we escape from His presence as soon as we can. We cut short our prayers, and our thoughts come back with a spring to our business or our pleasures as if we had kept them on God for a few minutes by force; also, when the Sabbath is a weariness, and secret communion with God is a hassle."

Alonzo felt that the pastor was describing his feelings, exactly.

"Also, it is evidenced when we hold back a little from cordial acquiescence in God's justice and in His fearful decision to punish sin, both as exhibited in His daily dealings with mankind and in the Bible. We shrink from some things in His administration, just as one condemned prisoner is shocked at what he calls the cruelty of the government in executing a convicted felon.

"Now do you, when examined by these tests, love God or dislike him?"

It was plain from the appearance of the assembly that they felt condemned. The pastor perceived that they pleaded guilty. He closed his remarks with these words: "You ought to love God. He commands you to do it. You should have loved him all your lives; you ought to love him now. He will forgive all the past for His Son's sake, if you will now simply turn your hearts to Him. Seek peace with your Maker without delay."

"I will do it," thought Alonzo, as they kneeled once more to offer their parting prayer. The pastor uttered expressions of penitence, gratitude, affection, but Alonzo perceived that, notwithstanding his determination, his heart did not follow. The more he tried to force himself to love God, the more clearly he perceived the distinctions which the pastor had been drawing, and the more painfully evident it was to him that he had no heart to love God. He rose from his knees with a thought, half impatience and half despair: "I do not love Him, and I cannot love Him. What shall I do?"

For many weeks, Alonzo was quite discouraged and distressed. He saw more and more clearly that he did not love God, and that he never had loved Him. Conscience upbraided him and he had little peace. Yet he would not come and yield his heart to his Maker. He thought he wished to do it, as if it were possible for a person to wish to love, without loving. He struggled, but struggling did no good. What God commands us to do is to love Him, not to struggle against our hatred of Him. He set a double watch over his conduct: he was more regular in his prayers, more attentive to the Scriptures, and to every means of instruction; but all seemed to do no good. His heart was still alienated from God, and it seemed to him to become alienated more and more.

There were three great difficulties which he experienced, and which perplexed and troubled him exceedingly.

First, it really seemed to him that he could not change his heart; he could not force himself to love God and repent of sin. He also could not help the wrong and wicked feelings which often raged within him, on occasions of peculiar temptation. I am aware that the theological philosophers disagree on this subject, but it really seemed to Alonzo that his wicked heart was too strong for him. This thought, however, did not make him comfortable. Conscience upbraided him the more for being in such a state of heart towards God.

Second, the more he thought of the subject, and the more he tried to make himself fit for heaven, the more hollow and superficial and hypocritical he found all his supposed goodness to be. The Law of God claiming his heart had come home to his apprehension, and brought a new standard before him. His supposed gratitude and penitence, his prayers, and all the virtues on which he had prided himself, resolved themselves into elements of corruption and sin under the powerful analysis of the Holy Spirit.

Third, in trying to correct his sinful habits, his progress in discovering his sins went on far in advance of his success in purifying himself from them, so that in his attempts to reform his heart he was continually alarmed at new and unexpected exposures. In fact, the Law of God had come home to him, and as oil upon the fresh surface of a variegated wood brings out the dark stains which had before been invisible, it exposed corruptions and sins in his heart which he had never supposed to be slumbering there. He was alive without the Law once, but when the Commandment came, sin revived and he died. His heart sunk within him as he saw his sad spiritual condition. In a word, Alonzo opened his eyes to the fact that the excellences of character which circumstances had produced in him were external and superficial, and that he was in heart the enemy of God and the miserable, helpless slave of sin.

Though he was thus, in some degree, aware of the condition of his heart, that condition did not alter. The trouble with him was that he still disliked God and loved the world and sin, but he feared a judgment to come. However, instead of throwing himself fully upon God and giving Him his heart, he still kept away, alienated and miserable. He had certain excuses with which he unconsciously deceived himself, and he was gradually lulling his conscience to rest. Then one day, he had a private interview with his pastor where he presented his excuses and they were answered. These excuses, and the replies made by the pastor to them, were in substance somewhat as follows:

"Sir, I do feel that I am a most miserable sinner, but I do not know what to do. I have been seeking religion for many years, and the more I seek it the further I seem to be from it."

"What more then, can you do?" said the pastor.

"I am sure I do not know," responded Alonzo.

"Then why does your heart fail to rest quietly in the consciousness of having been faithful to the utmost in duty? God requires no more."

Alonzo hung his head. He perceived the absurdity of his excuse.

"No," said his pastor, "you show by that remark how easily and completely the heart deceives itself. Upbraided as you are by conscience for guilt in disliking and disobeying God, reproached so severely and continually that you cannot rest, you yet say to me that which implies that you have done and are doing all which God requires."

Alonzo sighed. It was too true.

"I know it," he said. "It is just so. I continually find some new proof of the corruption and deceitfulness of my heart. I want to change it, but it seems to me that I cannot."

"You speak as if your heart were one party and you another;

and as if you were right, and all the blame rested upon your heart, as an enemy that had planted itself by some means into your bosom. Now what is your heart? It is simply yourself; your moral character and moral feelings. To talk of a contention between yourself and your heart is a complete absurdity, for the parties in the contest are one and the same thing. The struggle, if there is any, is between the claims of God's Law urged by his Spirit, on the one side, and you or your heart resisting on the other. He commands you to give him your heart – that is, yourself, your affections, and your love; yet you do not do it."

"I know it, but it seems to me that I cannot help it. I am conscious that my affections are not given to God; that they will cling to the world and sin, and I cannot help it," cried Alonzo.

"The feelings, however, which you cannot help, you admit to be wrong feelings," said the pastor.

"Yes sir, I feel and know they are wrong, and that is what makes me miserable."

"Then you are more guilty than I supposed. What should you say if you knew of a man who said that he had such an uncontrollable desire to steal or to kill that he could not help but continually commit these crimes? Should you think him worse or better than those who sinned occasionally under strong temptation?"

"But I struggle against the feelings, and cannot conquer them," said Alonzo.

"And suppose such a man as I have described should meet you in a lonely place, and should tell you that he must rob and murder you; that he had been struggling against the urge but it was too strong for him. What would you think of him?

Why plainly, that he was a man of extraordinary depravity. The greater the struggle, the greater the evidence of the wickedness which could not be overcome. Our duty is to feel right towards God, not to struggle with wrong feelings," responded the pastor.

"I feel that that is true. But what can I do to change? It does seem to me that I want to repent of sin and forsake it... but... but..."

"But you do not, and therefore it is impossible that you should want to. There is no force applied to you to make you continue in sin. If there was, your conduct would not be sin. To wish to repent, without repenting, is as impossible and absurd as to wish to be sorry for something for which you are really glad. I have no doubt you really think you wish to repent, but I think you deceive yourself. What you wish for is some of the results which you suppose would follow from repentance. This is what the desires of your mind rest upon; but repentance itself looks disagreeable and repulsive, and as you cannot gain those results in any other way, you are troubled and distressed."

Alonzo saw at once by a glance within that this was true. He longed for peace of mind, relief from the reproaches of conscience, the reputation and the standing of a Christian here, and assurance of safety and happiness hereafter; but he perceived that he did not long for penitence itself. It was a disagreeable means of obtaining a desirable end. He was silent for a few moments, and then he said with a sigh, "Oh, how I wish I could begin life anew. I would live in a very different manner from what I have done."

"That remark shows how little you know after all, of your own character and of the way of salvation. It is not by purifying ourselves, and thus making ourselves fit for heaven, or by any such ideas as should suggest the plan of beginning life anew.

If you should begin, you would undoubtedly be again as you have been," said the pastor.

Alonzo saw that this was true. He was ashamed that he had expressed such a wish, and at length asked, in a sorrowful desponding tone, whether his pastor could say anything to aid or guide him.

"I do not know that I can," was the reply. "The difficulty is not the lack of knowledge, but the lack of a heart to do it. If you had the right desires, your difficulties would all be over in a moment; but as you have not, I cannot impart them. Since you are thus bent on sin, God alone can change you.

"However," continued the pastor, "I will ask you one question. Do you clearly understand what this verse means: For they, being ignorant of God's righteousness, and going about to establish their own righteousness, have not submitted themselves to the righteousness of God; for Christ is the end of the law for righteousness to every one that believes."

"No sir, I have never thought of it particularly," said Alonzo.

"You feel in some degree the hopelessness of your condition if God should leave you to yourself. You have been neglecting your highest duty all your days, and in your efforts to seek religion you have been endeavoring to set yourself right with an idea of thus recommending yourself to God's favor. You have been discouraged and disheartened by this hopeless labor, for the farther you proceed in your efforts to repair your character, the more deep and extended do you find the proofs of its inherent corruption and depravity.

"You are like the man attempting to repair a house gone thoroughly to decay," continued the pastor, and as he said these words he took down from a little set of shelves behind him a small volume from which he read the following passage:

The sinner going about to establish a righteousness of his own, is like a man endeavoring to repair his house which had thoroughly gone to decay. When he begins there is a tolerably fair exterior. It appears as if a few nails to tighten what is loose, a little new flooring, and here and there a fresh sill, will render all snug again; and that by means of these, together with wallpaper and paint to give the proper superficial decoration, all will be well, or at least, that his building will be as good as his neighbor's. When he begins, however, he finds that there is a little more to be done than he had expected. The first board that he removes in order to replace it with a better, reveals one in a worse condition behind it. He drives a nail to tighten a clapboard, and it slumps into decayed wood behind, taking no hold. He takes away more, by little and little, hoping at every removal to come to the end of what is unsound, but he finds that the more he does, the more disheartened and discouraged he feels. His progress in learning the extent of the decay keeps far in advance of his progress in repairing it, until at last he finds to his disappointment that every beam is gone, every rafter worm-eaten and decayed, the posts pulverized by dry rot, and the foundation cracked and tottering. There is no point to start from for making his repairs; no foundation to build upon. The restoration of the edifice to strength and beauty can never be accomplished; if it could, the expense would far exceed his financial means. His building only looks the worse for his having broken its superficial continuity. He has but revealed the corruption which he never can remove or repair.

"Now does not this correspond with your efforts and disappointments during the last few months?"

"Exactly," said Alonzo.

"And your case is hopeless if God leaves you to yourself. You cannot be saved. It is not that you cannot come and be the child of God if you wish to, but you cannot come because you do not possess the will to love Him.

"Now, this being your condition, you need a Savior. There is one for you. If you wish, you can come and unite yourself with Him. If you do, through His sufferings and death you may be freely forgiven. The responsibility, the liability so to speak, for the past will be cut off. The Savior assumes all that burden and you may go free. By coming and giving yourself up wholly to Him you bring your past life as it were to a close, and begin a new spiritual life which comes from union with Him. The burden of past guilt is like a heavy chain which you have been dragging along until it is too heavy to be borne any longer. Union with Christ sunders it at a blow, and you go forward free and happy, forgiven for all the past, and for the future enjoying a new spiritual life which you will draw from Him. In a word, you abandon your own character, with the feelings with which a man would abandon a wreck, and take refuge with Jesus Christ who will give you the power to receive Him and procure for you forgiveness for the past and strength for the future, by means of His own righteousness and sufferings."

Alonzo had heard the way of salvation by Christ explained a hundred times before, but it always seemed a mysticism to him, as it always does to those who have never seen their sins and felt the utter hopelessness of their moral condition. As long as man is deceived about his true character, he desires no Savior. But when his eyes are opened by God and his deep seated corruptions are exposed, when he feels the chains of sin holding him with a relentless grip in hopeless bondage, then he finds that utter self-abandonment and humble reliance upon a Divine Redeemer whose past sufferings ransomed him, and who will supply new spiritual life to guide him in the future. He finds this prospect opens to him a refuge just such as he needs.

As Alonzo walked home from this interview, his heart dwelt with delight on the love of Christ to men in thus making arrangements for taking lost sinners into such an union with Him. His heart was full. There was no struggling to feel this love and gratitude. It was the warm, spontaneous movement of his soul which no struggling could have suppressed. He longed for an occasion to do something to evidence his gratitude. It was evening, and he looked forward with delight to the opportunity of calling together his family to establish family prayers. He almost wished that the exercise was twice as embarrassing as it was, for he longed to tell his family about the new spirit of love which burned within him, regardless of the consequences.

As he walked along, his heart clung to the Savior with a feeling of quiet happiness. In former days, he thought he loved Him; now he knew he did. He saw "God in Christ, reconciling the world unto Himself," and the Savior whom he saw there was all in all.

When he opened his Bible, old familiar passages which had always seemed strange and unintelligible to him, shone with new meaning:

"Christ has redeemed us from the curse of the law, being made a curse for us." "Being justified by faith, we have peace with God by our Lord Jesus Christ." "I am crucified with Christ, nevertheless I live, but the life I now live in the flesh, I live by faith in the Son of God, who loved me and gave himself for me."

Alonzo made greater efforts to do his duty after this than he did before, but it was for a different object and in a different way. Then, he was trying to establish his own righteousness, so as to fit himself for heaven. He abandoned this altogether now, having hope only in Christ — undeserved mercy in Christ. He made great efforts to grow in grace and to do good to others, but it was now simply because he loved to do it. Previously, he made these efforts as an unpleasant but a supposed necessary means to a desired end. Now, he hoped to secure that end in another way, and he made these efforts because they were delightful on their own account. He was, in fact, a new creature – a "new creature in Christ Jesus"; changed not by his vain efforts to establish his own righteousness, but by the regenerating influences of the Holy Spirit, altering fundamentally the desires and affections of his inmost soul.

Reader, in going forward through this volume (which will explain to you the way to do good) – if your aim is secretly or openly to fit yourself by your good deeds for the approbation of God, and thus to procure the pardon for your sins; the farther you go and the greater the effort you make, the more discouraged and disheartened you will be. Your progress in discovering the corruption and depravity of your heart will keep far in advance of your success in correcting or repairing it. The hopeless task may as well be abandoned in the beginning as at the end. Come first to the Savior. Give up yourself, your character, and all the hopes you may have founded upon it. Unite yourself with Christ as the branch is united to the vine; to be sustained by one common vitality. This will of course be a new life to you, a spiritual life without which all excellence is superficial, all hopes of eternal happiness baseless, and all real peace and enjoyment unknown.

Therefore being justified by faith, we have peace with GOD, through our LORD JESUS CHRIST.

WHICH HOPE WE HAVE AS

AN ANCHOR OF THE SOUL BOTH SURE & STEDFAST.

HEBREWS VI 19

THE SURE AND STEADFAST ANCHOR.

# Chapter 3

## How to Instruct Children for Eternity

Perhaps the reader had expected that the subject of religious instruction would have formed a substantial part of the last chapter. However, it is so extensive and important that it seemed better to give it a more full discussion in a separate chapter. Besides, the principles to be communicated now will apply not merely to the young. It is the whole question of approaching human intellect with Biblical truth that we shall here consider – whether the subjects be young or old.

The following propositions exhibit the view of the topic which we shall discuss in this chapter:

- The success depends upon the fullness and force with which the details of truth and duty are presented, not upon the scientific accuracy with which they are condensed into systems of theology.

- The Bible must be referred to as the great storehouse of moral and religious truth.

- The field of observation and experience must be explored for the means of applying and enforcing religious truth in the most meaningful manner.

- The admission of moral truth into the soul is to be secured mainly by means of a testimony awakened in its favor from within.

- Attempts to remove error by argument and personal controversy are almost always in vain.

These propositions we will proceed to consider in their order.

**The success depends upon the fullness and force with which the details of truth and duty are presented, not upon the scientific accuracy with which they are condensed into systems of theology.**

We are first struck by the remarkable difference between the mode which God has taken to instruct mankind in religious truth and duty, and that which in modern times we almost spontaneously fall upon. His mode and order of instruction are totally different from ours in at least one respect. He exhibits the principles of truth and duty, one by one, as they occur in connection with the ordinary events of life. We give them in the order of a well-digested and logical system. In fact, we might say that we teach the system, rather than the truths themselves, by whose arrangement the system is constituted.

God's first lesson to the human race was the first five books of Moses: the simple story of the patriarchs and of the children of Israel, and the institution of the moral and ceremonial law. Our first lesson would very likely have been an abridged, systematized, severe treatise on the science of moral and religious philosophy. He simply tells the story of Cain and Abel. We, perhaps, would have given a thorough explanation of the nature of murder, proving that human life is sacred. He narrates the history of Abraham, perhaps not using the word faith and certainly not making a single remark concerning its nature, from one end of the story to the other. We discuss the theory of faith, separate its essence, and point out all the distinctions in its varieties, some real, others imaginary. Religious duty, as God presents it, is a living and acting reality moving about among men, developing its character by its conduct. In our hands, the Bible lies upon an operating table, as some writer has justly said, and we are probing its inward structure with scalpel and forceps. The dissection is most ingenious and skilful and the demonstration, though sometimes lost in minute details, is still very scientific and complete; but then, the poor subject is often murdered and mutilated under the operation.

Still, we should be careful at this point, for we do not mean to altogether condemn the tendency to analysis and systemmaking, so prevalent in modern days. Instruction today has somewhat different objects and must pursue somewhat different means when addressed to individuals by one of us, from those adopted by Jehovah to the infancy of the human race six thousand years ago. We do not, therefore, compare the two methods in order to altogether condemn ours. We wish to look at both, for we may learn a good deal from either, especially as it is undoubtedly true that in our efforts with the young it will be best for us to incline strongly to the example which God has set for us in His own communications.

But a word or two more before we proceed, in respect to the nature of the difference just referred to. We can illustrate it by describing the modes in which two individuals might pursue the study of botany. One takes books of scientific arrangement, begins with classes and orders, and looks upon the whole vegetable kingdom as a scientific system. He goes into the field to collect specimens, simply as partial illustrations of the great artificial edifice which the labors of the botanist have gradually formed. The system (the arrangement and the classification), is all in all to him; the observed facts are only subsidiary and illustrative. It was not so with the botanists themselves when they first formed the system. The observed facts were the priority with them, and stood out prominent in their conceptions of the vegetable world. The system – the arrangement – came last, and was subsidiary and illustrative in respect to the facts. But our student has reversed this process. He begins where the botanists finished, and works back to where they began.

As an example, our second pupil goes out into the field looking for plants, and he first sees under the fences and by the roadside a clump of thistles. He examines the structure of this individual plant, noticing the leaf, flower, and seed. By means of books, or through his teacher, he learns to what degree the plant is extended over the earth (that is, what portion of the earth it occupies); whether it is spreading still, and if so, where and how; whether it is useful for any purposes, or dangerous to man and his environment; and whether methods are in use by agriculturists for its extermination, and if so, what they are. He examines minutely its structure: its leaves, its flower, its seed, and studies its habits. In a word, he becomes thoroughly acquainted with this one plant, a plant that is all around him, which he sees every day, and is often a subject of remark or conversation. While he has been doing this, the first pupil, who began at the other end, has perhaps nearly finished committing to memory the names of the various plant classes.

Our second pupil, upon mastering the thistle, perhaps takes the rose or some other common plant next. After having studied it thoroughly in its individuality, as he did the thistle, the teacher calls his attention to the points of resemblance, in respect to structure, which it may bear to the thistle. Here now is his beginning of system and arrangement; the connecting together by observed similarities the two objects with which, individually, he has become fully acquainted. This is beginning at the right end. This is really following on in the footsteps of the botanists, his masters. As he proceeds, he arranges and classifies his knowledge as quickly as he acquires it. System is thus the handmaid and preserver of knowledge, as she ought to be, and not the mere substitute for it. He builds up in his own mind the edifice of scientific system just as fast as the substantial materials are furnished him; and comes out at the end, as the great masters did before him, with that magnificent temple of science which, like all other substantial edifices, must be built from bottom to top, and not from top to bottom.

To make this case clear and distinct, I have represented the two modes, each pure in its kind. In point of fact however, there is ordinarily some mixture of the two, or rather, a general adoption of one course with some tendency towards the other. Intelligent teachers who may read this chapter will probably perceive that the principle of the latter mode, though really most philosophical in its nature, should not be pressed too far for the common purposes of instruction. The results arrived at by the original investigators of the science may aid the pupil very much in his efforts to follow them; the system and the principles of arrangement might very advantageously be explained in general.

Many teachers have erred in carrying to extremes the principle which I have been endeavoring to illustrate; in mathematics, for example, and in the natural sciences. They have sometimes pressed the plan of making the pupils pursue this natural course of induction so far, as to deprive them of the aid of those who have preceded them. In fact, carrying out the principle to its full extent would almost make every pupil an independent investigator and discoverer, whereas a normal lifespan would not provide the average student with the time to master any subject well.

The best strategy seems to be to let the pupil acquire knowledge first in detail, and then arrange and classify it as he proceeds. The worth and utility of what he learns will depend upon the fullness, freshness, and vitality of his individual acquisitions, and scientific system should be gradually developed as its apartments can be occupied. The building is beautiful in itself, it is true, but it is valuable chiefly as a means of securing and preserving from harm the valuables it contains.

We will now attempt to apply these considerations to the subject before us. Six thousand years ago, Jehovah began to communicate, by slow and simple steps, moral and religious truth to man. He brought forward these truths, not in the order of scientific system, but in that of commonness, everyday importance, and moral proximity. It is the thistle first, and then the rose. These revelations were slowly continued for many centuries. Throughout history, the most profound intellects and the purest moral sensibilities have been employed upon these truths, examining and arranging them, and noting the points of resemblance or diversity. They have examined them synthetically and analytically; they have made helpful distinctions, dissecting out truth into all its ramifications. They have also explored things most diverse and distinct in appearance and traced them to a common origin. These intellectual processes have been going on for ages. As a result, we have now before us the same truth which the prophets and the apostles taught, but arranged, classified, and formed into a scientific system.

Let now the reader not suppose that we mean to condemn this. Not at all. If anything is plain, it is that God intended that the minds of men should exercise themselves strongly and continually upon what He has revealed. The field of moral and religious truth, as contained in the Holy Scriptures, affords the finest scope for the exercise of the highest human powers. The nature of the case, and especially the very condition in which the close of His revelation has left mankind, shows plainly that He intended that we should explore and cultivate it. The object of these remarks is not at all to condemn theological science, but only to point out the facts with reference to their influence upon the course we should pursue, in endeavoring to instruct children in Biblical truth. That great mass of religious and moral truth, which the Bible and the human conscience bring before the mind in slow detail and minute applications, has been by patient theological labor and the accumulation of many centuries at last elaborated into scientific systems. We must not, in guiding the young, commence with the science and the system, and work back to the elements. Rather, we must start back at the beginning, giving them truth and explaining duty to them substantially in the order and manner in which God has done it, and move to the science and the system later on. We shall explain more particularly how this is to be done as we proceed. But this general view of the subject, if properly appreciated, will at once throw open a very wide field of Biblical instruction, and make the work comparatively easy.

Persons very often feel timid and constrained in their efforts at instruction in Bible class or with their own children at home because they feel that their own attainments are not of a sufficiently logical and systematic character. They understand vastly more than their pupils, but they feel that they are not scholars enough to teach what they know. They imagine that their own education has not been regular and systematic enough. However, the work they imagine they have to do is not the work to be done. As a parent, your simple business is to look around you at once, take anything that is moral truth, and then explain, expand, and exhibit it in its simplicity to the minds of the young. It does not matter whether your knowledge exists in the form of systematized theology or not. Your business is to bring before your pupils the elements, in all their endless application, to the circumstances and needs of common life. The theological system which you feel the need of, though it would be of immense value to you as a means of giving clearness to your conceptions and vigor and confidence to all your mental operations, is not after all what you want to present, as such, to the mind of the child. Teach them all the details of truth and duty in any logical order you wish. Study and present the principles of piety in their ordinary applications to the circumstances of life. Dwell on what is obvious, important, and of everyday usefulness, rather than on what is unusual or far fetched, and thus fill the minds of your pupils with the Scriptural truths which their future studies may classify and arrange. This is the wisest course for people who teach young Christians.

A brief word of caution is in order at this point, as we begin to move deeper into the discussion regarding how adults can best expose children to Biblical truth.

All individuals who are engaged in the noble work of imparting knowledge need to remember that children need more than knowledge; they need godly wisdom and humility. The chief goal in our efforts to educate young people must be to bring them to the point where their thinking and reasoning powers are profoundly influenced by Biblical principles. The master teacher, Jesus Christ, taught people by reasoning with them out of the Scriptures – not by overwhelming them with His intellectual superiority. In the same way, we must be careful to train children to filter all of their worldly wisdom through the truth of Scripture. Brute knowledge alone in the heart of a child will only puff him up with pride and cause him to be arrogant. Give a child knowledge <u>with</u> godly wisdom... this is the excellent way!

**The Bible must be referred to as the great storehouse of moral and religious truth.**

The doctrinal and historical portions of the Bible undoubtedly deserve a prominent place as the source from which religious instruction is to be drawn, but perhaps they should not occupy a share of attention so nearly exclusive as they often do. The Bible may be studied with many totally different objects and aims, each of which is valuable in its place. For example, we may carry a class rapidly over the books of Kings and Chronicles with the goal of obtaining a general knowledge of their literary contents; by collating them and comparing passage with passage, we may connect their chronological and historical details. Now this would be totally different from studying in detail the several narratives which these books contain in order to develop the moral lessons which each one was intended to teach. Scripture is an inexhaustible storehouse from which moral truth may be drawn – in every form of its development, and in all the innumerable varieties of its application.

Let us take a case to illustrate how the narratives of Scripture are full of moral truth. We will take Korah's mutiny, for example. We select this case because it is one of those narratives which is generally known to children. Therefore, it is suitable to our purpose of showing how much practical wisdom may be brought out, which otherwise would be passed by unnoticed and unknown.

The teacher in class or the parent at home opens the subject with the first verse of the passage, thus:

> Now Korah, the son of Izhar, the son of Kohath, the son of Levi, and Dathan and Abiram, the sons of Eliab, and On, the son of Peleth, sons of Reuben, took men; And they rose up before Moses, with certain of the children of Israel, two hundred and fifty princes of the assembly, famous in the congregation, men of renown. (Numbers 16:1-2)

In order to have the moral flow of the narrative clearly appreciated, the first thing is to consider distinctly the several parties in the transaction: Korah – one of the Levites, Dathan, Abiram, On, and their respective followers. In each case, we must observe both who the persons brought upon the stage of action are and what their situations and characters portray. We must recall to mind the arrangement which God had made with the Israelites in the wilderness. Aaron was the priest, holding the highest ecclesiastical dignity. The family of Levi came next, and the duties connected with all the ordinary services of worship rested upon them. The people were generally devoted to other occupations, too.

If the pupils now distinctly conceive of the vast assembly encamping in the wilderness – Moses the military commander, Aaron holding the supreme religious dignity, and the Levite Korah, uniting with the princes Dathan, Abiram and, On in a mutiny – they will be prepared to understand what follows.

> And they gathered themselves together against Moses and against Aaron, and said unto them, Ye take too much upon you, seeing all the congregation are holy, every one of them, and the LORD is among them: wherefore then lift ye up yourselves above the congregation of the LORD? (Numbers 16:3)

Much of human nature can be seen in this address. The real feeling in the mind of the speaker was, "I cannot bear to be second. I mean to stand as high in official dignity as Aaron." Ambition, pride, and a lack of submission to God were the stimuli of the speech. But how is the direct expression of it covered up and concealed? Found in the accusation against Moses and Aaron, and in a pretended vindication of the people's rights, is the universal excuse for the spirit of rebellion in every age: "You take too much upon you." They said this despite the fact that they themselves were going to take by usurpation the very same thing. Also, "all the congregation are holy," did not mean morally pure, but ceremonially competent in the eye of God to offer worship for themselves. This was said just as similar things are said now... to gain partisans. The aspiring demagogue, in order to carry on his schemes, always flatters the great mass which he wishes to move, telling them that they deserve an equality with the government which he desires to have them help overthrow.

Observe now an interesting coincidence which testifies strongly to the truth and faithfulness of this narrative. Who was the speaker in this case? There were two parties in the rebellion: Korah the Levite on the one hand, and on the other, Dathan, Abiram, and On from the people. So, which was the speaker? The narrative does not tell us directly, but the speech itself betrays the feelings of the Levite: "Ye take too much upon you, for all the people are holy," referring evidently to the ecclesiastical aspects of the arrangement they opposed. The reply of Moses corresponds. He spoke to Korah and all his company; therefore, we find that the lay leaders were not present.

How appropriate is the reply of Moses to Korah and his adherents; a stern rebuke was in order in such a case to clearly show their ingratitude and wickedness. After proposing a test where he would, on the next day, submit the question to the decision of God Himself, Moses reminds them of the high station to which they had been assigned and of the ingratitude and criminal ambition of aspiring to a higher one.

> Seemeth it but a small thing unto you, that the God of Israel hath separated you from the congregation of Israel, to bring you near to himself to do the service of the tabernacle of the LORD, and to stand before the congregation to minister unto them? And he hath brought thee near to him, and all thy brethren the sons of Levi with thee; and seek ye the priesthood also? (Numbers 16:9-10)

Moses does not reply to what Korah had said. He disregards the speech entirely and comes at once to the real source of the difficulty: the pride and ambition in Korah's heart.

Moses then sent for Dathan and Abiram. They refused to come, and instead sent a disrespectful message entirely different in respect to the grounds of the complaint (from Korah's speech); a message in exact keeping with the characters of the men. Korah's pretense was the natural one coming from an ambitious priest; that of Dathan and Abiram was just as natural from a discontented and rebellious people.

> Is it a small thing that thou hast brought us up out of a land that floweth with milk and honey, to kill us in the wilderness, except thou make thyself altogether a prince over us? Moreover, thou hast not brought us into a land that floweth with milk and honey, or given us inheritance of fields and vineyards; wilt thou put out the eyes of these men? We will not come up. (Numbers 16:13-14)

We will not go on any further with this narrative. But the following questions show how much moral truth such a narrative, when fully appreciated, may provide:

- In what did the sin of these men chiefly consist: the feelings, the words, or the actions?

- Did Korah commit any wicked act? Did Dathan and Abiram?

- Did they all commit mental attitude sin?

- What is the name for the kind of attitude they had?

- Do children ever demonstrate a rebellious spirit? Against whom? Do they ever feel the rebellious spirit when they do not manifest it in actions or in words?

- Can a rebellious spirit be expressed by looks as well as

by actions? Do children ever express it so? By what sort of looks?

• Is the rebellious spirit a pleasant or a painful feeling? Were Korah, Dathan, and Abiram probably happy while rebelling? Would they have been happy if they had succeeded in what they wanted to do?

The posing of questions like these might be the best way of bringing out the truth contained in this narrative, or suggested by it if the pupils are children. If the audience is mature, the same points would be brought to view, along with the same moral analysis of the story, though the results would receive an expression in language in a somewhat different manner. The questions we have listed above have by no means exhausted the subject. There are many other moral instructions to be deduced from the narrative. In verse eleven, for example, Moses considers the rebellion to be against the Lord. This naturally leads the mind to the consideration that Moses and Aaron, being appointed by God, were clothed with His authority, and that opposition against them was rebellion against God Himself. Properly illustrated and explained before children, this will set in a very striking light why a rebellious spirit against their parents, even if shown only by looks, or not expressed outwardly at all, is a sin not merely against their parents, but against God.

It is not that such a passage directly teaches all these truths or that they can be logically deduced from them, nor that it merely suggests them as principles to be proved. The narrative calls up the principles to the mind as principles intuitively perceived to be true. They are to be expressed by the voice of the teacher, knowing that the expression of them will be re-echoed and confirmed to the pupil by a voice within. There are, indeed, Biblical truths which must be proved, but we do not speak of them here. We speak now of a thousand principles of right and wrong that are brought to view in the narratives of Scripture and which need no proof. If you provide children with a chance to comprehend them, they will gain conviction. So in some respects, the story is the storehouse which the mind explores for moral treasures.

We have taken this single case, and dwelt upon it to show how minutely and fully the individual passages of Scripture should be explored as mines of moral and religious truth. I need not say that the whole Bible, examined thus, would furnish an inexhaustible store of wonderful learning. Praise God that His Word will never go out in vain, but will always accomplish His perfect will.

All persons, both old and young, will take a far greater interest in the moral aspects and flow of the Scripture histories than they will in the mere incidents of the narrative; or rather, the incidents of the narrative itself will excite interest in proportion to the moral meaning that is seen through them. Teachers of the young often overlook this. They bring Scripture narrative before their pupils simply as a history of occurrences, and a great portion of the force and beauty lying beneath the surface is not seen. In short, the Bible is not presented as a source of historical truth that is relevant to children today.

For example, take the story of Job. We may present it in two totally different ways to a class of little children. Suppose, for the first experiment, we gather the little pupils around us and read them the account of Job's prosperity, accompanying it with familiar explanations. We tell them how many sheep, oxen, and camels he had, and help them to picture in their minds some idea of his lifestyle, his vast herds, and his large household. Their curiosity, imagination, and wonder are strongly excited. Then you read to them the account of his successive losses. You describe the incursions of the enemy and the effects of the lightning, bringing home clearly to the minds of the pupils the terrific scenes alluded to in the description. The children are all intensely interested in it, as in a dreadful tragedy. At the end, perhaps, you say that Job did not curse God, notwithstanding all these calamities; he was patient and submissive, and we should all follow his example.

Thus the interest awakened in the minds of the children is an interest in the story, as a narration of wonderful incidents. The moral bearing of it is but slightly alluded to, and the whole impression made by it is upon the imagination, and not upon the heart.

We turn now to the opposite course, passing lightly over the incidents and bringing out fully the moral meaning of the story. You begin by telling, in general terms, of Job's vast possessions, and then point out that God determined to take them all away in order to try him; to see whether he would bear it submissively and patiently.

"Do you know what submissively and patiently means?"

A few children reply, "Yes, sir." "No, sir."

"Suppose one of you should have a beautiful picture book, and when you were sitting down to read it your mother said, 'Come, you must put that book away now. I want you to go to bed,' what do you think you would do or say?"

A pause.

"Perhaps you do not know exactly what you would do or say, but you may tell me what a bad child might do or say in such a case. Anyone may tell me."

Some of the children answer, "He might begin to cry." "He might say, 'I very much want to sit up a little longer.'" "He might say, 'I won't.'"

"Yet a boy who was patient and submissive would shut up the book pleasantly, bring it to his mother, and say, 'Very well.' Now, do you all understand what patient and submissive means?"

"Yes, sir."

"Well, then we will go on with the story of Job. God took away all his property in order to try him; to see whether he would be patient and submissive."

Next, read the accounts of the calamities by which Job was reduced to poverty. Explain it in such a way as to awaken their sympathy for him.

"Thus," you say in conclusion, "all his flocks and herds were carried away, his children were killed, and his servants taken captive or destroyed – all except the men who had escaped to tell him."

After answering some of the children's questions, he continues, "Yes, it is true that they were killed. Now, what do you think Job said? Do you know?"

"No, sir."

"It was something very remarkable. It showed at once if he was patient and submissive. It was very remarkable, indeed, for people have since repeated it a great many times when they have lost something which they value very much. It was this:

> The LORD gave, and the LORD hath taken away; blessed
> be the name of the LORD." (Job 1:21b)

A pause.

"It was just as if the child whose mother had taken away his beautiful book should say as he was going upstairs to bed, 'My mother gave me the book, and my mother has taken it away; I will not complain to my mother.' If he said this, don't you think he would be a patient and submissive youngster?"

Now in this case, it is plain that great effort has been made to bring out the moral expression of the story so that children can see and appreciate it. However, we have not detailed these two modes of explaining the same story to condemn the former; but rather, to only show how it is completely distinct in its nature. Both kinds of interest ought to be awakened. The latter, however, is especially important, for it alone gives the study of the Bible an influence on the affections of the soul.

The Bible is a great deep mine to be explored. Therefore, excite in your pupils as strong a dramatic interest in the narrative as you can, but let all of this interest be concentrated upon the moral principles of which the narrative is intended to be an expression. Moral training is best understood as the process of incorporating Biblical principles into the routine conduct of a person.

**The field of observation and experience must be explored for the means of applying and enforcing religious truth in the most meaningful manner.**

The habit of analyzing human conduct and character, and reflecting upon it, is absolutely necessary if we desire to command the avenues to the heart. We must be in the habit of noting the most common occurrences and tracing them back to the springs of action from which they rise. Observe the moral truths which they will illustrate or the moral principles they exemplify, and reflect upon them in your hours of meditation. In short, develop your power of spiritual discernment to the point where you recognize that when children engage in godly activities, it is the direct result of right thinking.

The attitude and manner of children says something of their character. The actions of a group of children at play often reveal the various propensities of childhood. Some people look at children playing and unfortunately see nothing in it but unmeaningful playfulness and confusion. Study children, and you will soon begin to understand more about their world, and their spiritual needs.

Using this principle to study children will give the Christian immense facilities for instructing his pupils in religious truth. He will, by such means, greatly extend his knowledge of this truth, in all its thousands of ramifications, and in its endless connections with the circumstances of life. Thoroughly furnished with a knowledge of the Scriptures he may go freely and boldly forward, and he will be prepared to labor in this field with the greatest success. The study of the Bible will give him the truth which he is to present, and his study of children will open to him the avenues by which he is to present it.

Human beings are frequently tempted to invest much of their time in worldly projects of one kind or another: building bridges, mowing lawns, painting houses, or pursuing a vocation. However, people do well to remember that time spent in God's Word and in the personal lives of people is the best possible investment. Bridges rust and fall down, houses pass away, as do jobs; but the Bible and the souls of men are eternal creations. Training a young soul for eternity is a wonderful privilege that should not be missed.

**The admission of moral truth in the soul is to be secured mainly by means of a testimony awakened in its favor from within.**

In several instances through the course of this work, we have had occasion to refer to the readiness with which moral and religious truth is received by the human mind when it is properly presented. There is a sort of moral intuition by which moral beauty and excellence are comprehended.

This would be true without limitation or exception, were it not for the influence of passion and sin which produce moral blindness and cut off the view of moral truth from the soul. The very way, however, by which these operate (in shutting any moral principles from the mind), illustrates what we have said; for they produce these effects, not by incapacitating the mind from following any trains of reasoning by which the principle might be sustained, but by rendering it insensible to its intrinsic excellence and beauty. Our great work, therefore, is to present truth rather than to prove it to man. We are to gain access for it around, under, over, or through the prejudices and sins which oppose its admission. Then we are to present it in its own intrinsic excellence and beauty, and exhibit it in its details and in its applications, confident that if it is perceived, it will commend itself and be established by its own intrinsic character, rather than by any train of calculation by which it may be shown to result logically from established premises.

This is true in regard to a great many cases which at first might appear as exceptions. There is, for example, the evidence of the truth of Christianity. We are accustomed to see it presented in a well-connected train of argument, which proceeds from what is admitted as premises to the result finally arrived at as conclusion. But it is not the force of it which generally determines the faith of Christians, nor does it even materially affect that faith. The true ground on which Christianity is received, where it is really received, is a perception of its moral features by a mind spiritually sensible of them. It commends itself to the moral needs of the soul, and when the Holy Spirit causes someone to see his spiritual needs, Christianity is received in quick order. In other cases, Christianity is not really believed. The education or the habits of the individual may be such that he does not choose to deny its truth, but he does not really receive it; the argument, at least, does not convince him.

Moral truth may sometimes be proved by the adduction of facts, or by the results of experiment. But this is a very slow and toilsome process. "Facts," it is said in a common proverb, "are stubborn things." To this it has been very properly replied that they are the most flexible, uncertain things that the human intellect has to deal with. Even in the physical world, it is far more difficult to establish any truth by a legitimate induction. Do the various positions of the moon, in her monthly revolution, affect the changes of the weather? To settle such a question by a series of observations, made with accuracy and perseverance will require a vigilance which those who are not accustomed to philosophical inquiries would be slow to anticipate. In the moral world, the difficulty is incomparably greater. Though it is very often the case that writers attempt to prove the wisdom of plans, or the efficacy of measures for the promotion of piety by an induction of facts, these facts are seldom sufficient to establish the point.

It is pleasant to reflect how close at hand God has placed all the moral and religious truth necessary for human salvation. If labored reasoning had been necessary to establish it, how many millions, even in a civilized and Christian land, must have lived and died in hopeless ignorance; but God has provided better for the needs and dangers of humanity. He has so adapted the constitution of the human mind to the immutable and eternal principles of right and wrong, that our great work is simply to manifest them in order to have them received; and where they are rejected, it is sin, not intellectual incapacity, that causes their exclusion.

**Attempts to remove error by argument or personal controversy are almost always in vain.**

Sometimes when we argue, we are not arguing with error at

all. We aim directly at the establishment of the truth, and that without supposing any tendency to error in our hearer. As when, for example, one young man presents to another the evidence in favor of the immortality of the soul, which he may have collected; not as a means of combatting his errors, but of confirming and establishing his belief in the truth. Parents often argue like this with their children, and pastors with their people. They attempt to prove the truth, feeling all the time that their hearers go along with them easily, wishing to have it proved. It is obvious that there are few dangers or difficulties here, since the speaker and hearers are agreed. They are travelling a road which they all wish to travel; the followers looking up to the leader as a guide. Under such circumstances, there must be some extraordinary clumsiness to create any difficulty on the pathway to agreement.

Again, in other cases, we argue not for the truth but against error, while our hearers are still unbiased and willing to be led wherever our arguments may carry them. Here there is a little greater danger than in the other case, for error is dangerous to meddle with in any way.

First, there is danger that our mere statement of the error will introduce it, in accordance with the principle that we have often alluded to (in the course of this work), that statements have more influence generally upon the human mind than reasoning. An idea presented will often enter and remain, bidding defiance to all the exorcisms of argument and appeal by which the introducer of it attempts to get it out again in vain. Second, by the violence with which we assail an opinion and its advocates, we may create a sympathy in their favor and lead our hearers to take their side, on the principle which leads us often to side with the absent and undefended – whether right or wrong. Thus, while we imagine that our hearers are admiring the havoc our intellectual cannon is making in the battlements of the enemy, they are in fact secretly stealing over to the aid of the fortress assailed. In these and similar ways we may, while combatting error, enlist some of the feelings of human nature in its favor, feelings stronger than allegiance to logic and reasoning. These dangers, however, serious as they are, must not now be dwelt upon; rather, a third case must be presented.

We sometimes argue directly with those holding erroneous opinions. This is what we intend by the phrase "attempting to remove error by argument," placed at the head of this part of the chapter. Here lies the greatest difficulty and danger. The attempt to convince young people of error is the most delicate and hazardous of all the modes of action of mind upon mind. By saying it is delicate, I do not mean that it is a nice operation. The forces are not small and weak, requiring nice attention and adjustment to develop them. They are, on the contrary, great and uncontrollable. There is the mighty power of truth on one side, and the still mighty power of error on the other. There is habit with its iron chain, prejudice and passion with their swift current, pride with its strong walls, and falsehood and inconsistency with their heaps of rubbish. These you have to overcome and remove. Indeed, you have on your side the clear, silent light of reason and the voice of conscience, powerful enough to conquer anything else; but pride, passion, and habit will conquer them.

When the speaker has a willing listener, his work is easy; but when he has to lead one along in a way in which he does not wish to go, his work is all but hopeless. Established opinions are sometimes changed, but not often by reasoning. New associations, the slow influence of altered circumstances, the change effected in the whole character of the soul by real conviction of sin – these and similar causes, affecting the feelings more than the reasoning powers, often subdue pride, break down obstinacy, and undermine long established errors. The brute power of reasoning, it must be acknowledged, moves a person to change only on rare occasions.

Still, there are many cases where argument helps to hasten the abandonment of error (although, perhaps, it as often only confirms its dominion). Despite all this, many persons, especially the young, are eager to engage in it. Experience generally gives us more sober expectations of success from it, but in early life we are ready for the combat. By faithfully studying, understanding, and adopting the following four principles, our readers will avoid many of the dangers of such conflicts, and will somewhat increase the faint hopes of leading children out of error.

First – Fully understand the position taken by the child whose errors you wish to correct. To do this, you must go to him, as it were, and see with his eyes. Remember that error appears reasonable to all who embrace it. It is a fictitious reasonableness, I grant, but it appears real. Now you must see this yourself, or you cannot understand the light in which the subject stands and the mind you are endeavoring to reach. If, instead of this, we keep at a distance and develop expressions of frustration at a child's errors and of astonishment at his inconsistency and wickedness in holding them, we may gratify our own self-righteousness and spiritual pride, but we can do him no good.

"Father," says a little child, sitting on his chair by the fireside on a winter evening. "Father, I see a light, a strange light outside, over across the road."

"Nonsense, you silly child, there is no house across the road, and there can be no light there this time of night."

"But I certainly see one, father – a large bright light."

"There can be no such thing," insists the father. "It cannot be so. There is nothing over there that can burn. I can see out of the window myself, and it is all a white field of snow."

This is one way of combatting error. The boy is silenced but not convinced, and were he not awed by parental authority, he would not even be silenced.

Another father, in a similar case, responds by saying "Where?" From his own chair he can see the field and across the road. He sees nothing, so he goes to the child, puts his eye close to his son's, and says, "Where? Let me see? Ah, I see it. Well now, walk slowly with me up to the window."

Thus he leads the boy up and shows him the grounds of his illusion in a reflection of the fire from a pane of glass.

Now, this is the proper way of correcting error. You must first see it as the child whose opinions you wish to correct sees it. Patient investigation of another's views can also save embarrassment in cases where we discover that another party is correct after all! Now, you can do your young friend no good: you cannot sympathize with him, you cannot understand him, and you cannot advance a step in reasoning with him, unless you first go and put your intellectual eye where his is.

It is no matter what the opinions are against which you contend; you cannot contend against them to advantage unless you understand them. If any opinion seems preposterous and absurd to you, the probability is that you could, by discussion, do no good to the individual who holds it. It is plain that it does not appear preposterous and absurd to him; therefore, the perception which you attack is not the one which he maintains. It may be the same in name and somewhat the same in substance, but in all those aspects and relations of it which constitute its life and give it its hold upon him, it is different to you from what it is to him, and your discussion will be an angry dispute in which neither will understand the other.

If, therefore, a young man, in referring to any error such as

Atheism, Deism, or disbelief in a judgment to come, said, "It seems utterly astonishing to me that anyone can believe such an error. I do not see what he can possibly be thinking. I would like to meet with the person holding this belief, for it seems to me I could show him his mistake." If he said this, it is pretty safe to infer that he would act most wisely by letting the error alone. He does not understand it. In a discussion, he would not make the slightest progress. There would be a violent collision between him and his unbelieving opponent, from which each would recoil in a sort of maze.

If, however, he says, "I do not think it surprising that such a man should be a Deist. Considering his education, his associates, and the position he occupies, I can easily see how the subject of revealed religion should present itself in such a way to his mind as to lead him to disbelieve it." If he says that, there is a little more hope. There is some ground for sympathy. The discussion can have a beginning, and if there can ever be hope of any progress, it is in such a case.

No one, therefore, can be qualified to attempt to lead any young soul out of its errors, unless he first listens to them. Perhaps you will shrink from doing this. It requires you to go over to the side of error and look upon it with favorable eyes, and this is dangerous. It is, perhaps, the most dangerous work which we can engage in. If the reader should consider his hope of bringing any youngsters out of the wiles of error too feeble to justify his incurring the hazard of going in there after them, to be, perhaps, lost himself, I should most sincerely approve of his caution. But then, if he is deterred by this danger from qualifying himself suitably for the work, he must not undertake it. He can do nothing but exhaust and irritate himself, and fix his young friend in his delusions by attempting to argue without proper understanding.

Second – You must not only go to the intellectual position which your friend occupies in order to begin the discussion, but you must keep with him all the way. You draw him out, as the magnet draws out the iron, by keeping in contact; the moment you break from him, you lose him. You can do nothing at a distance, for arguments have little weight unless the heart is open to receive them; candor, good humor, and intellectual sympathy are necessary in order to keep the heart open.

Now, the moment you enter into conversation with a young friend upon a subject on which you disagree, it is very hard to avoid an argument. Generally, the course of things is that as soon as anything like discussion is commenced, each party recedes as far as possible from the other, and by exaggeration, overstatement, and pressing to extremes, they get to as great a distance as they can. From these positions, which they have respectively taken, they shower one another with angry words, each gravely expecting to drive the other over to himself. In some cases of moral conversation between mind and mind, there may properly be a separation, or a lack of sympathy; like when a child is rebuked for a known and admitted sin or denounced for opinions which carry on the face of them their own condemnation. Nevertheless, we must do more than simply point out error. In our efforts to remove the demon of error, we must not only remove the demon, we must also replace the error with solid truth; and this takes time and patience.

You must be careful not to overstate any fact or exaggerate the force of any consideration which is in your favor, nor underrate anything which your antagonist may advance. Be honest and candid. Admit the force of objections and difficulties. Listen attentively to what he says, not as a mere matter of formality, but from an honest desire to know exactly how the subject stands in his mind. Do not be in haste to reply to what he says, but admit its force and take it into consideration. Thus he will perceive that your object is not victory but truth, and as you show yourself willing to look candidly at the whole subject, he will by sympathy catch the same spirit, and you will thus go on together. As long as you can keep together you may perhaps advance, but the moment you separate, he falls back and your hold over him is gone.

Third – Avoid rousing your young friend, by opposition, to take ground in defense of his opinions. If you wish to fix a youngster most firmly on either side of any question, the surest way is to give him that side to defend. Hence, the great danger and evil of discussions is that they become disputes and make each party more fixed and obstinate than before. Therefore, avoid putting your friend upon his defense, or making an antagonist of him. You can do nothing with an antagonist. If he sets forth an argument or states a fact, do not reply to it or contradict it; instead, by an honest question or two, draw it out more fully so as to completely possess yourself of it as he sees it. If it is weak, do not make him think it strong by putting him on the defense of it. If it is strong, do not impress it upon his memory and give it undue importance by arguing about it. In either case, trust to the great leading considerations which you have to introduce as the means of overcoming its influence.

With the greatest circumspection, you may find it all but impossible to prevent your conversation from degenerating into a dispute. You may read and understand these principles now, and admit their reasonableness. But when you come to apply them, you will find an almost insurmountable difficulty. In fact, the reader will be very likely to say (while reading these paragraphs), that the rules are very good in theory, but impossible to keep in practice. I grant it – or at least I believe it is almost impossible to preserve them. It is certainly very difficult, in endeavoring to convince a young person of the erroneousness of his opinions, to avoid arousing him to a resolute defense of them. This is no doubt true, and yet there is still reason to hope for some success if we focus our efforts on presenting basic truths instead of arguing against error.

Fourth – Make it your great object to present to your friend, and to keep before his mind, those great leading considerations on which evidence of the truth must rest, and not to discuss with him the details, difficulties, and objections which cluster around every great subject. It is but a few great considerations which determine the conviction of the mind in all cases. The truth of Christianity rests on its great, visible, moral effects; not on the details of that complicated argument which researches into its history have furnished, nor on the possession of satisfactory answers to the thousand objections which have been advanced. It is, indeed, very important to possess these answers since there are certain occasions and certain purposes for which they are significant. But in such discussions as we are speaking of here, the more exclusively the mind that is wrong is brought to look upon the great leading considerations which establish the truth, the better.

We are prone to overrate the extent to which it is necessary that the many difficulties and objections, which can be raised against the truth, should be met and answered. They must to some extent remain, for the mind is full of them on every subject. All truth, whether believed or disbelieved, is connected with difficulties which we cannot remove. The most common doctrines of philosophy (such as, that sound is produced by areal vibrations, that cold is the mere absence of heat, and many of the other most questionable truths), are encompassed with difficulties which are very hard to solve. The best approach for a wise instructor to take is not to call attention too much to these questionable areas.

In religious discussion, we should do the same. Our great object is to bring forward the leading considerations which balance the scale and determine conviction; and then to present these to the mind, making as little reply as possible to the counter considerations. By doing this you gain double advantage: you secure the presentation of what must be the basis of conviction, if it is established at all, and you avoid the most imminent of dangers; putting the child upon the defense of his opinions which would inevitably confirm him in them.

These principles, if understood and practiced, will perhaps aid a little, but in the end, we can promise the private Christian very little success in his efforts to do good by reasoning with error. There are a thousand difficulties and obstructions which prevent gaining access to the human soul. Some of these obstacles are: pride, the power of habit, the influence of association, authority, interest, and the bias of feelings averse to the sacrifices which sound moral principles require. Truth and logic, with all their power, are often frail instruments among such immoral forces as these.

Ultimately, in a fallen world like ours, we cannot trust in the expectation that the truth will necessarily make her way if we simply arm her with intellectual weapons and send her out to fight against error. The result of such conflicts will generally depend more upon the ability of the advocate, or rather upon upon his personal influence, than upon the goodness of the cause. Our job as Christians is to speak the truth in love, and leave the results to God.

In conclusion, this chapter relates mainly to personal discussion between private Christians in the ordinary walks of life; not to controversy among leading minds advocating diverse opinions before the public. There are times when Christians must publicly argue for the truth, even if the public fails to listen; however, this book is not intended to address that topic. The sphere of influence in which this book is designed to move is a different one altogether. In that sphere there can be no question that disputation should hold but a very low rank among the means of doing good. Our means of promoting the spread of Christianity is to spread its gentle and noiseless influence. We are to exhibit it in our lives. We are to explain, enforce, and exemplify its duties. We are to express its principles and gain an influence for them among our fellow men. Thus the frequency of arguments will be lessened, and the moral influence of an alluring exhibition of the principles and duties of holiness will find an easy way, where the most severe and scientific theological arguments for the truth would find every access barred and impregnable.

These remarks apply with particular force to modern paganism and humanism. They prevail to a vast extent in the world and must continue to prevail for some time; and although the proof of the Truth ought to be constantly before the community so as to be accessible to every mind, to rely upon the logical force of arguments, as the main instrument for the expulsion of ungodliness, is to altogether mistake the nature of its power. Ungodliness, as it has generally shown itself in this world, is not candid philosophical doubting of the mind; it is rejection by the heart. Its strength is not in its reasonings but in its spirit. It is dislike toward God, penitence, humility, and a communion with heaven. It is love of this world and of sin, and a determination to go on its own way without fear of a judgment to come. It is a spirit of hostility toward God and to His reign, and a determination not to submit to it. Now logic and reasoning can never change such a spirit; they do not even tend to change it. Reasoning with young people, therefore, must not stop at the mind; it must go straight to the heart by way of consistent, gentle, and Biblically based training.

### RULES OF BEHAVIOR

Adults can use the following list to help youngsters understand what good behavior is in many circumstances of life. Remember, children need to be taught how to incorporate Biblical morality into their day-to-day real life circumstances.

1. Every time you are in the company of others, you ought to show some sign of respect to those present.

2. Do not sing to yourself with a humming noise, or drum with your fingers or feet, in the presence of others.

3. Do not sleep when others speak, sit when others are standing, or speak when you should keep quiet. Do not walk away from someone who is speaking to you.

4. Do not try to joke or play with someone who does not feel like playing. Do not lean on or touch another person unless they give you permission.

5. Do not read letters, books, or pages in the company of others. If you have something urgent to read then ask your visitors to give you a few moments to go into another room for reading purposes. Do not read another person's letters, unless asked. Do not look over another person's shoulder when they are trying to write.

6. When someone is speaking, be attentive and do not disturb the audience. If the speaker is having trouble forming words, do not try to help him unless you are asked to help. Do not interrupt a speaker, or ask him questions, until his speech is ended.

7. Stay away from people who constantly speak about other people behind their back. Do not get into the habit of prying into the private life of any person.

8. Be thankful for the food that is set before you to eat, whether it be large or small. Do not find fault with the cooking that others do on your behalf. It is very improper to lean on the table when you eat. Do not grab food from the table in a greedy manner; rather, let other people take their food before you start to eat.

9. If you visit someone who is sick, do not try to play the physician unless you have training as a doctor. Always

speak the truth plainly, using the Bible as your guide. A
sick or lonely person should not be told a false report
about their condition. False hope breeds misery.

10. It is improper and arrogant to try to teach someone to do
    something that they already know how to do.

11. Do not push people into giving up secrets. Gossip is the
    sport of fools.

12. If two or more people are arguing with each other, do not
    seek to take sides until you are sure you know all the facts.

13. Do not start arguments at the dinner table. Good humor
    makes any meal a wonderful feast.

14. Give honor to whom honor is due. Render respect to those
    who are in authority regardless of their birth. Be sure to
    take off your hat and open the door for all women, as well
    as men.

15. Respect your elders at all times. Permit them the first
    chance to speak when in their company.

16. In writing or speaking, give to every person his due title,
    according to his degree and the custom of the place.

17. When you give someone else advice, be sure to give it in a
    spirit of modesty. Do not be quick to point out another
    person's faults.

18. When you speak of God or His attributes, let it be
    seriously, in reverence. Never use God's name, unless it is
    for the purpose of worship, praise, or godly instruction.

19. Give honor to your parents for God's sake, though they
    may be at times poor and cruel.

20. In your clothing, be modest and endeavor to accommodate nature, rather than to procure admiration. Keep to the fashion of your equals if they are civil and orderly with respect to times and places.

21. Do not play the peacock – looking everywhere about to see if you are well decked, if your shoes fit well, if your stockings set neatly, and if your clothes impress other people.

22. Think before you speak and pronounce carefully; God will require each person to answer for each word spoken.

23. Do not make a habit of promising to do things that are beyond your normal ability to perform. When you make a promise, be sure you can keep it.

24. Make sure that you are organized when you give a speech. Do not bounce from one subject to another or repeat often the same matter.

25. Let your general daily attitude be pleasant, but in serious matters somewhat sober.

26. Never use bad language against anyone. Do not curse or revile them.

27. Do not mock or jest at anything of importance. If you happen to say something funny or pleasant, do not laugh at your own humor.

28. If you care to develop a good name and reputation, be sure to choose companions that have a godly character; for it is better to be alone than in bad company.

29. Never rejoice at another person's calamity, even when there seems to be some cause. To avoid looking foolish, be sure to laugh only when there is just cause.

30. Give advice to others only when they ask for it to be given. Do not visit or stay at a place where you are not welcome. Be sure that you do not take undue advantage of another person's kindness.

31. Do not state that something is true if you are not sure of the source. In sharing information with others, be slow to release the name of the author, for some information is better kept secret.

32. When a person does all that he can do to succeed in a noble endeavor, and yet fails, do not blame him for trying. Commend someone who has done a good deed, but do not engage in excessive flattery.

33. Do not envy the blessings of others. God gives to all that honor Him more than they deserve.

34. Do not whisper to another person when you are among company. Furthermore, what you speak in secret to your friend, deliver not to another person's ears.

35. Fear God and keep His commandments, for this is the whole duty of man. Moses brought down from Mount Sinai the Ten Commandments, not the Ten Suggestions.

*(These rules of behavior were written by our nation's first president, George Washington, at the age of thirteen.)*

# Chapter 4

## Teaching Children to Be Happy

It is often assumed that all children know how to be happy. In reality, however, few children are ever provided with the understanding they need regarding how to be happy. The following directions should be shared with young people in the order in which they are presented. If adults will take the time to share with children the principles contained in this chapter, they can save many young people from life's most common pitfalls.

First of all, what I mean to say to the reader, in respect to this part of my subject, is this. If you wish to be happy – if you wish to have any real peace, any steady and substantial enjoyment – you must make up your mind decidedly whether you will be the child of God or not. If you expect Him to take you under His care, you must be his: really, honestly, and thoroughly, not merely in pretence and in form. If you find, therefore, that in looking into your heart you are not happy, it is very probable that the cause may be that you are not really and fully at peace with God. You have only declared a truce, and then recommenced hostilities. Of course you cannot expect to enjoy a quiet and a happy heart. You may, however, depend upon the fact that your days must be days of uneasiness and misery until you come and make yourself wholly the Lord's. To secure your happiness then, your first duty is to most faithfully and thoroughly examine your spiritual condition, to confess and to crucify your dearest sins, and to cast yourself upon the merits and atonement of your Savior. Then you will be prepared to go on to the next step.

The next step in the order of importance, is to see that all your worldly affairs are in order. The special power of system in increasing success has often been praised, but it has, if possible, a still greater power to promote happiness.

People talk about the cares of business, the perplexities of their daily lot, and the endless intricacies in which they find themselves involved; but they are, nine times out of ten, the cares of mismanagement and the perplexities of confusion. The burdens of human life are often doubled, and sometimes rendered ten-fold greater than they otherwise would be, because people are unorganized. The proof of this is that when a man, either from some natural discipline of the mind or the effect of early education, acquires the habit of order and method, he can accomplish more than twice as much as ordinary men; and of all the men in the community, he is most likely to have time for any new and sudden call. Now, if he can do twice as much, with no more care and hurry, it is plain that he could perform the ordinary work of man with a far more quiet and peaceful mind. This is unquestionable. The facts are notorious, and the inference from them immediate and irresistible.

But let us look more particularly at the manner in which disorganization and confusion, in the management of worldly business, affects the peace and happiness of the heart. There are few persons so correct in this respect that they will not find a testimony within them to the truth of what I shall say. Let us take the following case as the basis of our illustration.

James is a school boy. His affairs, though not quite so intrinsically extensive and important as those of an accountant, are still important to him. He has his business, his cares, his disappointments; the conditions of success and happiness are the same with him as with all mankind.

James' first duty in the morning (I speak only of his worldly duties here), is to rise at six o'clock and start a fire in his father's wood-burning furnace.  James hears the clock strike six, but it is cold, and he shrinks from his morning's task; he lies still, postponing the necessary effort.  His mind is all the time dwelling upon it and dreading it, and his conscience goading and worrying him with the thought that he is doing wrong.  Thus fifteen minutes pass most wretchedly.  The mistake he makes is in imagining two evils:  a little sensation of cold on his face and limbs while dressing, and the nagging of a disturbed conscience.  So he quietly waits, suffering the latter for fifteen or twenty minutes, until the lapse of time makes it too intolerable to be borne any longer, and then he slowly forces himself out of his bed.  He then finds that he still has to bear the first evil after all.  Instead of taking the least of the two evils, he has taken both, and the bitterest first.

Many of my readers will condemn James' folly – but be not in haste.  Do you never in any way procrastinate duty?  Look over your mental memorandum, and see if there is anything upon it that you have been putting off because you have been dreading it.  If so, you are like James completely.  He who procrastinates duty which he knows must be done, always chooses both evils, beginning with the bitterest portion.

James has in fact chosen three evils, for the recollection of this neglect of duty will continue all the morning.  For hours there will be an uneasiness in his mind, whose cause and origin he may not distinctly understand, though he might find it if he would search for it.  He feels restless and miserable, though he knows not exactly why.

When James comes down to his work, he finds no proper preparation made.  The wood which should have been carefully prepared the evening before is out under the snow.  The fire has gone out and his tinderbox cannot be found.  He did not remember where he had left it, so of course he has to search for it at random. When he finds it, the matches are gone, the flint is worn out, and only a few shreds of tinder remain. Perplexed and irritated at the box, instead of being penitent for his own sinful negligence, he toils for a long time; and at last meets with partial success in kindling his morning fires, an hour after the proper time. The family, however, does not distinctly call him to account for his negligence, for the family which produces such a character, will generally be itself as shiftless as he. Still, though he expects to sustain no immediate accountability, he feels uneasy and restless, especially as he finds that his postponed and neglected morning's work is encroaching upon the time he had allotted to his morning's school lesson.

For James is a school boy, and the lesson which he is to be called upon to recite, as soon as he enters school in the morning, he had postponed from the evening before. It ought to have been studied during the half hour before breakfast, which he expected that he should find. Acting without a plan and without goals he is, of course, disappointed; and when he rises from his breakfast table, he seems surprised to find that it is time for school to begin. He hurries away to find his books, hat, and coat, for every morning they have to be found. He goes about the house with angry feelings, scowling brow, and fretful tone, displeased with everybody and everything except the proper object of displeasure – himself.

He hurries to school. It is a bright and beautiful winter morning, and everything external tends to either calm the mind to peaceful happiness or to awaken emotions of joy. But James cannot be happy. Even if he should now begin to be faithful in duty, it would be many hours before the turbulent sea of commotion which he has raised in his heart would subside. He is worried, restless, anxious, and unhappy. He sees the external circumstances in which he is placed as the source of his sufferings, instead of looking for their cause within.

I need not follow him through the day. Everyone will see that with such habits, he must be miserable. And yet James is not a bad boy, in the common sense of the word. He has few vices. He will not steal. He will not lie. He loves his father and mother, and never directly disobeys them or does anything intentionally to give them pain. Perhaps my readers would be surprised to have me tell them that he is a Christian. He is, nevertheless, a sincere Christian. He has repented of his sins and made his peace with God, and he lives in the daily habit of communion with God. In his hours of retirement and prayer he experiences many seasons of high enjoyment, and yet he generally leads a very wretched life. A constant, irritating uneasiness corrodes his innermost soul, and he knows not why. In fact, he seldom inquires why. He has borne it so long and so consistently that he has no idea that serenity, peace of mind, and steady happiness are within the reach of the human soul in this world. Thus he goes on, accomplishing very little and suffering a great deal. Now the reader must remember that it is the suffering that we are now considering; our object is not to show how a lack of discipline and organization interferes with success in life, but how it destroys happiness.

Very many of my readers will probably find, by careful examination of themselves, that though their circumstances and condition may be totally different from those of James, their characters are substantially like his. Disorder, irregularity, and perhaps confusion reign in your affairs. Instead of acting on a general plan, having your business well arranged, your accounts settled, and your work in advance, you act from impulse and temporary necessity. Instead of looking forward – foreseeing duty and providing for its claims, regularly and methodically – you wait until it forces itself upon you, and then waste your time and your spirits. You neglect or postpone unpleasant duties, leaving them to burden your mind and mar your peace and happiness, until at length you are forced to attend to them because some new thorn of irritation pricks in your side.

# Training Children in Godliness

Parents can help to discipline their children in the important character trait of orderliness by providing them with routine work responsibilities. They should see that the duties that are assigned to their children are performed satisfactorily. In short, do not protect children from work. It is far better and easier to help youngsters develop responsible work habits when they are young, instead of trying to correct such habits when they are already employed outside the home. This advice is very practical, for if we fail to reform our children's character and work habits, they will rarely be addressed by our children's employer — except perhaps by discharging the worthless worker from the payroll!

So, whatever may be the reader's situation and condition in life, if he wishes to be happy, let him regulate his affairs. If you have uncertain, unsettled accounts open, which you have been dreading to examine, go and explore the cases thoroughly and have them closed. If there are plans which you have been intending to accomplish, but which you have been postponing, summon your resolution and carry them at once into effect, or else determine to abandon them and dismiss them from your thoughts.

The mind of a young and ardent man becomes loaded with crude, half-formed designs, unfinished plans, and duties postponed. He is like a child unaccustomed to the world, who takes a walk on a pleasant summer's day. Every object seems valuable, and he picks up a pebble here, a stick there, and gathers a load of pretty flowers in this place and that, until he becomes so encumbered with his treasures that he can hardly go on. They are constantly slipping and dropping from his hands, and become a source of perplexity and anxiety to him because he cannot retain them all. So it is with us. Every plan which reason forms or imagination paints, we think we must execute; but after having made a new beginning, a new project which we are equally eager to secure enters our heads. In a short time, we become encumbered with a mass of intellectual lumber which we cannot carry and are unwilling to leave. Consider what you can and will execute, and take hold of the execution of them now. Abandon the rest, so that you may move forward with a mind that is free and uncluttered.

This, then, is the second great rule for securing personal happiness. Look over your affairs, and arrange and methodize everything. Define in your own mind what you have to do, and dismiss everything else. Take time for reflection, and plan all your work so as to go on smoothly and quietly so that the mind may be ahead of all its duties, choosing its own way, and going forward in peace.

There is one point in connection with this subject of the management of worldly affairs which should not be passed by, and which is yet an indispensable condition of human happiness. I mean the duty of every man to bring his expenses and his financial liabilities fairly within his control. There are some cases of a peculiar character, and some occasional emergencies, perhaps, in the life of every person, which constitute exceptions; but this is the general rule.

The plentifulness of money depends upon its relation to our expenditures. A big city banker with an annual income of $200,000, may be pressed for money, and be harassed by it to such a degree as to make life a burden; while a common laborer on a railroad in New England may have a plentiful supply with only eighty dollars a day, in the dead of winter. Reduce your expenditures, your style of living, and your business far below your financial means, so that you may have money in plenty.

Perhaps there is nothing which so grinds the human soul and produces such an insupportable burden of dependency as financial pressure. Nothing more frequently drives men to suicide. There is, perhaps, no danger to which men in an active and enterprising community are more exposed. Almost all are eagerly reaching forward to a station in life a little above what they can well afford, or struggling to do a business a little more extensive than they have capital or steady credit for. Thus all through life they keep just above their means; and just above, by even a small excess, is inevitable misery.

If your aim is happiness, reduce your style of living and your responsibilities of business to such a point that you shall easily be able to reach it. Do this, I say, at all costs. If you cannot have money enough for your purposes, in a house with two rooms, take a house with one. For there is such a thing as happiness in a single room, with plain furniture and simple fare; but there is no such thing as happiness, with responsibilities which cannot be met and debts increasing, without any prospect of their discharge. If your object is power, the credit of belonging to good society, or the most rapid accumulation of property, and you are willing to sacrifice happiness for it, I might perhaps give you different advice. But if your object is happiness, then this is the only way.

The principles which we have thus far laid down, as the means of attaining personal happiness, relate to both young people and adults. Let us be quick to share this time-proven and biblically sound advice on the subject of happiness with our families – our children in particular.

Before we bring this chapter to a close, we will consider one more primary means that adults can employ to increase the happiness of children.

### Every Child Needs a Home

It is all too often forgotten that children need a loving, disciplined home if they are to be happy. The God-ordained institution of the family was deliberately developed by God to increase the level of happiness in human beings. Now parents very often go to great lengths to increase the happiness of their children through the purchase of fancy and expensive toys, while very often neglecting what may be their children's most important physical need: a solid Christian home.

The fact is plainly clear today that Christian parents can no longer afford to take any aspect of the institution of the family for granted. There simply is no other social institution that can hold a candle to the family.

God intended for mankind to dwell in happy and loving union together. There is double enjoyment in family love: the pleasure of giving affection, and the pleasure of being the object of it. It is hard to tell which is the greatest. A man will sometimes neglect his family that he may increase more rapidly his wealth or influence in the world. However, he makes a sad mistake to barter his interest in some project, for the richer, deeper emotions of happiness which might be secured by loving and being loved by family members.

God has grouped men in families, having laid the foundation of this institution so deep in the very constitution of man that there has been no nation, no age, scarcely even a single savage tribe, that has not been drawn to the result which He intended. For thousands of years, this institution has been assailed by every power which could shake it by violence from without, or undermine it by treachery from within. Lust and passion have risen in rebellion against it. Atheism has again and again advanced to the attack, but it stands unmoved. It has been indebted to no human power for its defense. It has needed no defense. It stands on the firm, sure, everlasting foundations which God has made for it. Wars, famine, pestilence, and revolutions have swept over the face of society, carrying everywhere confusion, terror, and distress. Time has undermined and destroyed everything which it could touch, and all human institutions have thus been altered and destroyed in the lapse of ages. But the family lives on; it stands firm and unshaken. It finds its way wherever human beings go. It survives every shock, and rises again unharmed after every tempest which blows over the social sky. It is a contrivance for human happiness, and God has laid its foundation too deep and strong to be removed.

The current number of homeless children in America continues to grow and probably will for some time to come. Millions of youngsters sit in orphanages, hoping and dreaming to be adopted into a "real family." How sad it is that many of God's people have failed to understand how wonderfully the institution of the family is designed for the work of youth evangelism. Still, God is on the move, and may well be pleased to wake up more adults to see that the institution of the family is His great gift to mankind, especially designed to advance the happiness of all His children.

The following words of Scripture should encourage any person who is committed to teaching others about the Word and will of God:

> *Seek ye the LORD while he may be found, call ye upon him while he is near:*
>
> *Let the wicked forsake his way, and the unrighteous man his thoughts: and let him return unto the LORD, and he will have mercy upon him; and to our God, for he will abundantly pardon.*
>
> *For my thoughts are not your thoughts, neither are your ways my ways, saith the LORD.*
>
> *For as the heavens are higher than the earth, so are my*

*ways higher than your ways, and my thoughts than your thoughts.*

*For as the rain cometh down, and the snow from heaven, and returneth not thither, but watereth the earth, and maketh it bring forth and bud, that it may give seed to the sower, and bread to the eater:*

*So shall my word be that goeth forth out of my mouth: it shall not return unto me void, but it shall accomplish that which I please, and it shall prosper in the thing whereto I sent it.*

*For ye shall go out with joy, and be led forth in peace: the mountains and the hills shall break forth before you into singing, and all the trees of the field shall clap their hands.*

*(Isaiah 55:6-12)*

"HOME IS A SHELTER FROM THE WINTRY BLAST."

*George Herbert.*

# Chapter 5

## Teaching Children the Royal Law

One word that virtually all young people will hear numerous times during their childhood years is the word love. Although the word love is one of the most frequently used words in the English language, its meaning is often misunderstood or perverted.

It is a mistake to assume that children understand the significance of the word love, simply because they hear it spoken on a regular basis. Parents today must teach their youngsters what it means to walk in love.

As we begin to consider the topic of Christian charity, it is important to stress the fact that love it pre-eminently something we do, not merely something we feel. It was Jesus who said, "If you love me, you will keep my commandments."

This view of the doctrine of love is well summarized by Christian author, George Grant, in his book entitled *Bringing In the Sheaves*. On pages 45-48, Mr. Grant writes:

> The Good Samaritan is the unnamed lead character in one of Christ's best-loved parables (Luke 10:25-37). When all others, including supposed men of righteousness, had skirted the responsibility of charity, the Samaritan took up its mantle. Christ concluded the narrative, saying, "Go and do likewise" (Luke 10:37)...
>
> ...God desires all of us to display the Good Samaritan faith... The testimony of Scripture is clear: All

of us who are called by His name must walk in love (Ephesians 5:2). We must exercise compassion (2 Corinthians 1:3-4). We must struggle for justice and secure mercy, [as well as provide comfort] and liberty for men, women, and children everywhere (Zechariah 7:8-10).

In Matthew 22, when Jesus was asked to summarize briefly the Law of God, the standard against which all spirituality is to be measured, He responded, "You shall love the Lord your God with all your heart, and with all your soul, and with all your mind. This is the great and foremost commandment. And the second is like it; you shall love your neighbor as yourself. On these two commandments depend the Law and the Prophets."

Jesus has reduced the whole of the Law, and thus, the whole of faith, to love. Love toward God, and then, love toward man. But, at the same time, Jesus has defined love in terms of Law. In one bold, deft stroke, He freed the Christian faith from subjectivity. By so linking love and Law, Christ has unclouded our purblind vision of both. Love suddenly takes on responsible objectivity while Law takes on passionate applicability.

This sheds a whole new light on what is meant for us to "walk in love." If our love is real, then it must be expressed; it <u>will</u> be expressed. If our love is real, then action will result because love is something you do, not merely something you feel. Love is the "Royal Law" (James 2:8).

## THE PRINCIPLE OF BIBLICAL CHARITY

This chapter is intended to persuade the reader that the impulse which should lead Christians to the performance of charitable works in this world, is not a hope of fitting ourselves by meritorious performances for God's service in heaven; but a spontaneous love for God and man, urging us forward in such a course while our hope of forgiveness for sin rests on other grounds altogether. (The only remedy for sinful man is to trust in the substitutionary work of Christ on Calvary.) Some other considerations in respect to the motives which should influence us as we seek to love others shall be presented in this chapter as well.

By engaging in the work of Christian charity, we do not by any means sacrifice our own happiness. Indeed, we often give up some ordinary means of enjoyment, but we do not sacrifice the end. Rather, we secure our own richest, purest enjoyment, though in a new and better way.

We also change the character of our happiness, for the pleasure which results from carrying happiness to the hearts of others is very different in its nature from that which we secure by aiming directly at our own. Now the reader should consider these things, and understand distinctly at the outset whether he is in such a state of mind and heart that he wishes to pursue the happiness of others, or whether he means to confine his efforts to the promotion of his own.

On some cold winter evening, perhaps, you return from the business of the day to your home, where I will suppose that you have the comforts of life all around you. You draw up your richly stuffed elbow chair by the side of a glowing fireplace, which beams and brightens upon the scene of elegance which your livingroom exhibits. A new and entertaining book is in your hand, and fruits and refreshments are by your side on a table. Here you may sit hour after hour, enjoying these means of comfort and happiness, carried away by the magic of the pen to distant and different scenes, from which you return now and then to listen a moment to the roaring of the wintry wind or the beating of the snow upon your windows. If you have a quiet conscience, you may find much happiness in such a scene — especially if gratitude to God as the giver of such comforts, and as your kind Protector and Friend, warms your heart and quickens your sensibilities. Here you may sit hour after hour, until Orion has made his steady way through the clouds and storms of the sky, high into the heavens.

But, though this might be enjoyable, there is another way of spending an hour of the evening which would also afford enjoyment, though of a different kind. You lay aside your book, trundle back your cushioned chair, pack your fruit and refreshments in a small basket, and take down from your bookcase a little favorite volume of hymns. Then, muffling yourself as warmly as possible in cap and coat, you venture forth in the midst of the stormy night.

The brick sidewalk is half hidden by the drifts of the snow, among which you make your slippery way until you turn onto a narrow sidewalk, guiding your steps to one of its humble houses. You enter by a low door. It is not, however, the abode of poverty. There is comfort and plenty under this roof; though on a different scale from that which you have left at home, it is not inferior in respect to the actual enjoyment they afford.

The mother who welcomes you is a widow, and the daily labor of her hands procures for her all that is necessary for her needs, and much besides, which she enjoys as luxuries. She enjoys them more highly than you do the costly splendors you have left. Her bright, brass lamps, which she toiled several days to earn, and the plain rocking chair in the corner, are to her as much, and far more, than your fancy chandelier with its cut glass crystals, or your splendid ottoman.

In a word, all the needs of this family are well supplied, so that I will not introduce the reader to a scene of abject poverty, as you may have supposed. You must bring something more valuable than money here if you wish to do good. You have something more valuable than money – Christian charity. This I will assume you have brought.

On one side of the fire is a cradle which the mother has been rocking. You take your seat in a low chair by its side, and leaning over it you look upon the pale face of a little sufferer who has been for many months languishing there. His disease has curved his back, brought his head over towards his breast, and contracted his lungs; he lies there in bonds which death only can sunder. Something like a smile lights up his features to see that his friend came again to see him, even through the storm. That smile and its meaning will repay you for the cold blasts which you encountered on your way to the sick room. After a few minutes conversation with the boy, you ask if he would like to have you walk with him a little. He reaches up his arms to you, clearly pleased with the proposal, and you lift him from his pillow – and you enjoy yourself more, than even he does. The relief he experiences in extending his limbs, cramped by the narrow dimensions of his cradle, begins his happiness.

You raise your arms. He is not heavy. Disease has diminished his weight, and you walk back and forth across the room with a gentle step, his head reclining upon your shoulder. The uneasy, restless expression which was upon his face is gradually changed for one of peaceful repose; until, at length, lulled by the gentle sound of your voice, he drops into a quiet slumber. You may walk with him frequently across the floor, before fatigue will counterbalance the pleasure you will receive in watching his placid and happy look reflected in the glass behind you when you turn.

Eventually he wakes, and you gently lay him down into his cradle again. You read him a hymn expressive of resignation to God and confidence in His kind protection. Kneeling down by his cradle and holding his hand in yours, you offer a simple prayer in his behalf. And when at length you rise to go away, you see his countenance and feel the spontaneous pressure of his little hand, telling you that his heart is full of happiness and gratitude. In witnessing it, and in recalling the scene to your mind in your cold and stormy walk home, you will experience an enjoyment which I cannot describe, but all who have experienced it will understand. This enjoyment is very different in its nature from the solitary happiness you would have felt at your own fireside. Which kind, now, do you prefer?

True, the case I have described is an experiment on a very small scale. The good done was very little; it was only a half hour's partial relief for a sick child, and another half hour's happiness for him afterwards, as he lies in silence and solitude in his cradle thinking about the kindness of his visitor. This is truly doing good on a small scale, but then it is made by just a small effort. It illustrates well, because of its being so simple a case, the point to be illustrated: that you may take two totally different modes to make a winter evening pass pleasantly, and it is not merely a difference of means when the end is the same, but a difference in the very end and object itself.

"But is not the end sought in both cases our own happiness?" you ask.

"No, it is not." And this leads me to a distinction, an important spiritual distinction which everyone who wishes to perform charity on the basis of right principles should understand. The distinction is contained summarily in the following propositions. I hope my reader will pause and reflect upon them, until their meaning is distinctly understood. Then, he will be ready to enter into the spirit of the remarks which follow. The propositions are elementary, for they lie at the very foundation of Christian love.

- One may do good for the sake of the credit or the advantage of it, in which case it is a matter of policy.

- He may do good for the sake of the pleasure of it. Here it is a matter of feeling.

- He may do good simply for the sake of obeying God and from the desire to have the good done. In this case, it is a matter of principle.

**One may do good for the sake of the credit or the advantage of it.**

This choice is the secret of a far greater proportion of the apparently benevolent effort which is made in the world, than is generally supposed. I do not by any means say that it is wrong for a person to desire the good opinion of others, and especially to wish to be known as a person of kind feel-ing for the needs and sufferings of others. This is probably right. The degree, the extent, to which this operates upon us as a stimulus to godly duty is the main point we need to consider.

There are various ways in which this principle may operate. You may go and visit the sick, carry comforts to the poor, and be very active in your efforts to gather Sunday school scholars, or you may distribute tracts or collect contributions for charitable purposes. Doing these things, you pass along from month to month, imagining that your motives and feelings are all right. Still, if you were ever to pause and reflect, and call your heart thoroughly to account, you would find that your real stimulus is the wish to be esteemed by all your Christian acquaintances as an ardent and a devoted Christian, or as an active, efficient, successful member or manager of a charitable society. Or, you may contribute money – alas! How much is so contributed because you know it will be expected of you. The box or the paper comes around and you cannot easily escape it. You do the good, not for the sake of having the good done, but to save your own reputation. Or, to take another case still, on a larger scale, one more gross in its nature, you may (if you are a man of business and wealth), take a large share in some costly, charitable enterprise, with the design of enlarging your influence or extending your business by the effect which your share in the transaction will produce upon the minds of others. It is true that this feeling would not be unmixed. You would look, and try to look, as much as possible at the benevolent object to be completed; and a deceitful and desperately wicked heart would try to persuade you that this is your sole, or at least your principle, desire. If, however, you were suddenly laid up with a fatal illness, and could look upon these transactions in the bright spiritual light which the vicinity of another world throws upon all human actions and pursuits, you would see that in these cases you are doing good, not for the sake of pleasing God by doing His will, but to promote in various ways your own private ends.

Let it be understood that we do not say that this would be wrong, nor do we say it would be right. We say nothing about it. How far, and into what fields, a just and proper policy will lead a person in the transaction of his worldly affairs is not now our business to inquire. The subject we are considering is not policy but benevolence, and the only point which we wish here to carry is to persuade the Christian, who is commencing his course of godly action, to discriminate; to understand distinctly what is benevolence and what is not, and to have his mental and moral powers so disciplined that when he really is doing good for the sake of the credit of it, he may distinctly know it.

**He may do good for the sake of the pleasure of it.**

Doing good from the impulse of sentimental feeling is regarded among men as of a higher moral rank than doing good from policy (though it might be a little difficult to assign a substantial reason for the distinction). One of the lowest examples of doing good from mere feeling, is where we make effort to relieve pain because we cannot bear to see it. A wretched looking child, with bare feet and half naked bosom, comes to our door in a cold inclement season of the year. He comes, it may be, to beg for food or clothing. We might never have thought of making any search in our neighborhood for suffering people, but when such an individual intrudes himself upon us, we cannot bear to send him away with a denial. We give him food or clothing, or perhaps money; but our chief incentive for doing it is to relieve a feeling of uneasiness in our own minds. We do not say that this is wrong. All we say is that it is not acting from principle. It may be considered a moral excellence that the mind is so constituted in respect to its powers and sympathy with others that it cannot be happy itself while an object of misery is near, and the happiness of knowing that all around us are happy may be a type of enjoyment which it is very proper for us to seek. But still, this is doing good from feeling, not from principle.

Feeling will often prompt a charitable man to make efforts to promote positive enjoyment, and to relieve mere suffering which forces itself upon his notice. You "get interested," as the phrase goes, in some poor, unhappy widow and her children. The circumstances of her case are such, perhaps, as at first to make a strong appeal to your feelings; and after beginning to act in her behalf, you are led on from step to step by the pleasure of doing good until you have found her regular employment, relieved all her needs, and provided for the comfort and proper education of her children. All this may be right, but it may be simply feeling which has prompted it. There might have been no steady principle of benevolence through the whole case.

**He may do good simply for the sake of obeying God and from the desire to have the good done.**

There is a far wider difference between the benevolence of

principle and the benevolence of feeling than Christians may realize. Principle looks first to God and His law Word. She sees Him engaged in the work of promoting universal holiness and happiness. Not universal holiness, merely as a means of happiness, but holiness and happiness; for moral excellence is in itself a good, independent of any enjoyment which may result from it. Thus, principle has two distinct and independent, though closely connected objects, while feeling has but one. Principle deliberately decides to take hold as a cooperator with God in promoting the prosperity of His kingdom. She does not rush heedlessly into the field and seize hold of the first little object which comes in her way. Instead, she acts upon a plan, and surveys the field. She considers what means and resources she now has, and what she may, by proper effort, bring within her reach. Principle aims at acting in such a manner as shall in the end promote, in the highest and best way, the designs of God. She feels, too, that in these labors she is not alone. She is endeavoring to execute the plans of a superior, and she endeavors to act, not as her own impulses might prompt, but as the laws and principles of the Bible dictate.

Doing good from motives of policy, the first of the inducements we have considered, is unlikely to find much favor with human hearts if it can be simply deprived of its disguise. But, the distinction between feeling and principle demands more careful attention. The two may sometimes cooperate. They do very well together, but feeling alone cannot be trusted with the work of Christian charity. She can aid and inspire principle, and enable her to do her work better, but she cannot be trusted alone.

We can more clearly show the distinction between the benevolence of principle and of feeling by an allegorical illustration. Let us suppose that one evening, Feeling and Principle were walking on a road, along the outskirts of a country town. They were returning from an evening service in a schoolhouse, a mile from their homes. It was a cold winter evening, and as they passed by the door of a small cabin with boarded windows and broken roof, they saw a child sitting at the door crying bitterly.

Feeling looked anxious and concerned.

"What is the matter, my little fellow?" asked Principle, with a pleasant countenance.

The boy sobbed on.

"What a house," said Feeling, "for human beings to live in. But I do not think anything serious is the matter. Let us continue."

"What is the matter, my boy?" asked Principle again, kindly. "Can you tell us what is the matter?"

"My father is sick," replied the boy, "and I don't know what is the matter with him."

"Listen," said Feeling.

They listened and heard the sounds of moaning and muttering within the house.

"Let us continue," said Feeling, pulling upon Principle's arm, "and we will send somebody to see what is the matter."

"We should go and see ourselves," said Principle to her companion.

Feeling shrunk back from the proposal, while Principle, with female timidity, paused a moment, from an undefined sense of danger.

"There can be no real danger," thought she. "Besides, if there is, my Savior exposed himself to danger in doing good. Why should not I? Savior," she whispered, "aid and guide me."

"Where is your mother, my boy?" she asked.

"She is in there," said the boy, "trying to take care of him."

"Oh, come," said Feeling, "let us go. Here, my boy, here is some money for you to take to your mother." Saying this, she tossed down some change by his side.

The boy was wiping his eyes and did not notice it. He looked up anxiously into Principle's face and said, "I wish you would go and see my mother."

Principle advanced towards the door, and Feeling, afraid to stay out or to go home alone, followed.

They walked in. Lying upon a tiny bed covered with dirty and tattered blankets was a sick man, moaning and muttering and snatching at the blankets with his fingers. He was evidently struggling with a high fever.

His wife was sitting on the end of a bench by the chimney corner, with her elbows on her knees and her face upon her hands. As her visitors entered, she looked up at them. She was the picture of wretchedness and despair. Principle looked glad, but Feeling was sorry they came.

Feeling began to talk to some small children who were shivering over the wood-burning furnace, and Principle approached the mother. They both soon learned the true state of the case. It was a case of common misery, resulting from the common cause. Feeling was overwhelmed with painful emotion at witnessing such suffering. Principle began to think what could be done to relieve it, and to prevent its return.

"Let us give her some money so she can buy some wood and some bread," whispered Feeling, "and go away. I cannot bear to stay."

"She wants kind words and sympathy, more than food and fuel, for present relief," said Principle. "Let us sit with her for a little while."

The poor sufferer was cheered and encouraged by their presence. A little hope broke in. Her strength revived under the influence of heart-felt concern, which is more powerful than any medicated beverage; and when, after half an hour, they went away promising future relief, the spirits and strength of the wretched wife and mother had been a little restored. She had smoothed her husband's horrible cough and quieted her crying children. She had shut her doors, and was preparing to enjoy the relief when it should come. In a word, she had been revived from the brink of despair. As they walked away, Feeling said it was a most heart-rending scene, and that she would not forget it as long as she lived. Principle said nothing, but guided their way to a house where they found one whom they could use to carry food and fuel to the cabin, and take care of the sick man while the wife and her children sleep. They then returned home. Feeling retired to rest, shuddering lest the terrible scene should haunt her in her dreams, and saying that she would not witness such a scene again for all the world. Principle kneeled down at her bedside with a mind at peace. She commended the sufferers to God's care, and prayed that her Savior would give her some such work to do for Him everyday.

Although a very simple case, this is the difference between feeling and principle. The one obeys her own impulses, and relieves misery because she cannot bear to see it; the other obeys God. Because of this difference in the very nature of their benevolence, many results follow in respect to the character of their efforts.

First of all, feeling is unsteady. Acting merely from impulse, it is plain that she will not act unless circumstances occur to awaken the impulse. She, therefore, cannot be depended upon. Her stimulus is from without. It arises from external objects acting upon her, and so her benevolence rises and falls as external circumstances vary. The stimulus of principle, on the other hand, is from within. Hers is a heart reconciled to God as Lord, consistently united to Him with the desire to carry forward His plans. Consequently, when there is no work before her, she goes forth of her own accord and seeks work. She is, therefore, steady.

Second, feeling will not persevere. When she sees suffering she feels uneasy, and to remove this uneasiness, she makes gracious effort. However, there are two ways that she can choose to deal with suffering. She will cease to feel uneasiness not only when the need is relieved, but also when she becomes accustomed to witnessing it. She feeds a starving child, not because she wished the child to be happy, but because she cannot bear to see him wretched. Now, when she becomes accustomed to seeing wretchedness, she can bear it easily enough; therefore, she cannot continue with any extended benevolent effort. Before long she becomes accustomed to the suffering and it ceases to affect her; thus, her whole impulse, which is her whole motive, is gone.

Feeling is also inconsiderate. What she wishes is not to do good, but to relieve her own wounded sensibilities. She will give a needy person money at the door, though she might know that he uses the money chiefly as the means of getting that which is the chief cause of his wretchedness. That is, however, of no consequence to her, for the particular misery she encountered will be out of her sight; her purpose is answered equally well, whether the misery is relieved, or only removed from view. Therefore, she is inconsiderate. She is acting with gracious intentions, but often increasing the evil she intended to remedy.

Fourth, feeling aims only at relieving visible wretchedness. Indeed, if she was wise, she might aim at promoting general happiness on an enlarged plan, for her own enjoyment would be most highly promoted by this. But she is generally not very wise, and while principle forms plans and makes systematic efforts to promote the general enjoyment, feeling continues in a state of moral inaction with respect to the work of doing good, unless there is some specific and obvious suffering to be relieved.

Lastly, feeling does not aim at promoting holiness or diminishing sin, on their own account. Principle considers sin an evil, and holiness or moral excellence, a good. She considers them on their own account, independent of their connection with enjoyment or suffering. She would rather have all men grateful, obedient to God, and united to one another, even if they were to gain nothing by it in respect to happiness. Feeling does not take this view of the subject. Nothing affects her but the sight or the tale of woe. If you can show her that sin is the cause of some suffering which she is endeavoring to relieve, she will perhaps take an interest in endeavoring to remove it as a means of accomplishing an end. But in respect to the universal reign of love to God and love to man, because of the intrinsic excellence of love, she feels no interest. She does not perceive this moral excellence. She may be herself entirely destitute of this love and blind to the true duty that God has for each of His children.

In these respects, and in many more connected to them, principle is very different from feeling.

The reader will I hope, clearly understand the distinction between policy, feeling, and principle, as the chief motives in doing good. The question will naturally arise, at least it should arise: What is the character of our own benevolent effort? We shall all find that these motives are mixed in our hearts, and by a careful self-examination, we shall probably perceive that policy has more influence than either of the others. By policy I do not mean a deliberate intention to pretend to be generous to accomplish a sinister design; I mean doing good, with some real interest in it, but where the paramount inducement, after all, is the light in which the affair will be viewed by others. This may not be always wrong, as we have before remarked. A man ought not to be indifferent entirely to his own reputation. The favorable regard of the wise and good, everyone should desire, and it is right to take pleasure in the sense of its possession. But there are probably very few who would not be surprised, if they were to see their good deeds honestly analyzed. Such people would often see that a large part of their inducement during charitable activities was to be seen by men.

To discriminate between the benevolence of feeling and that of principle requires still greater care. The distinction is not exactly one between right and wrong, for to be influenced in our efforts by feeling is surely not wrong. We should feel deep compassion for the sufferings of others, and a great personal pleasure in the work of alleviating them. But principle should be the great basis of all our efforts at doing good. It is the only stable basis, and it is the only one which in any degree enables us to fulfill our obligations as the children of God. Doing good on principle is the only type of benevolence which is pleasing to Him.

If we wish to know which of these motives control us, we must pause when we intend to make some effort to do good. We must allow our thoughts to go freely forward and see what the object is on which they will rest, as the end to be secured. When, for example, you are making efforts to prepare yourself for your duties as a Sunday school teacher, in what is it that your heart rests upon as the object you are pursuing? Let your imagination go forward, beyond your present preparation; follow her and see where she goes – what picture does she form? Does she exhibit to your eye the beautiful appearance of a full and an attentive class, to be noticed by the other teachers, the superintendent, or by some individual friend whose good opinion you particularly want? Does she whisper to you the praises of your fidelity and your success, or does she warn you of the reproof or the censure, secret or open, which you must expect if you are unfaithful? Or, does she lead you to the hearts of the children, and show you renewed, sanctified affections there? Does she picture to you their future lives, purified from sin, and lead you to expect through them the extension of the Redeemer's kingdom?

So when a friend calls upon you, to ask your subscription to a charity for example, and you sit listening to the story, determining whether to add your name to the list, what is it that your imagination reposes upon at the instant of decision? Is it the satisfaction of the applicant at finding you ready to aid, the sight of your name by those to whom the paper is to be circulated, or relief from the pain awakened by the sad details of the story? Or, is it the pleasure of obeying God and aiding in doing His work? What is it in such cases that your mind rests upon at the moment of decision? Recall a few such cases to mind, give the reins to your heart, and see where it will go. If you take off all restraint and let it move freely, it would run to its own end, and there repose itself upon the object it is really seeking.

Ultimately, the Christian who wishes to love others the way God intended must act upon principle. He must come and give himself up to his Maker's service and aim at carrying out all His plans. He must first strive to bring men back to their allegiance to God, since without this every other plan for promoting human happiness must fail. Then he must do all he can to promote the present enjoyment of all God's creatures, in every way in his power. He must love happiness on a small scale, and on a large scale. He must wish that those all around him should enjoy themselves now, and a thousand years hence; and a thousand years hence, as well as now. This benevolence must reign so constantly in the heart, as to give a habitual character to the feelings, an expression to the countenance, and tone to the voice. The cooperator with God must also speak in the same language to all around him, especially to those in his own family.

This, then my reader, is the work which you must do, if you wish to cooperate with God. These are the objects you must aim at, not merely now and then, when some details of suffering intrude themselves upon your mind and awaken a temporary feeling, but steadily and constantly, as the great business of life. Your own happiness will be much promoted; however, your aim in pursuing these objects must not be your own happiness, but rather the accomplishment of the objects themselves – extending the reign of holiness, and fulfilling your duty as a grateful and obedient child of God.

## Teaching Children the Royal Law

Until Christ comes, let us be given to love and hospitality. Our fiery devotion to spread Christian charity will light the way for our children and inspire them to dare great exploits for King Jesus.

*My little children, let us not love in word, neither in tongue; but in deed and in truth. I John 3:18*

JUST AS THE TWIG IS BENT·

THE TREE'S INCLINED.

# Conclusion

It is hard to imagine a more wonderful privilege than that of training youngsters for eternity. However, nurturing children in godliness is not only a privilege, it is also a responsibility. It is precisely at this point where most adults, especially parents, experience the greatest problem. From the point of man's fall into sin until today, men and women have consistently struggled against the responsibilities that God has placed upon them.

In America, the latter portion of the twentieth century has given rise to a spirit of hedonism and humanism. An alarming number of parents in America have become lovers of pleasure more than lovers of God, and this attitude of heart has manifested itself in many ways. As far as the training of children is concerned, self-centered parents simply do not feel that God will hold them accountable if they choose to neglect their children's training in the things of God.

Notwithstanding this paganistic philosophy, the Bible teaches any adult who is sincerely interested in pleasing God that there are horrible consequences for those who "offend" children (see Mark 9:35-42).

More Christian parents need to be reminded that it is just as disastrous to neglect a child's training as to actively mistrain a child away from Christ.

The primary purpose of this book has been to provide parents, and other concerned adults, with important insights into the proper methods for turning a child's heart to God.

This advice will be totally worthless, however, unless the

reader makes it his or her responsibility to act upon the information that he has read.  In short, a "well-intentioned" parent is little better than a "pitifully neglectful" parent – and is probably no more successful in the long run.  Good intentions are no substitute for good actions and a faithful commitment to godly child training.

May God forgive all that has been wrong, either in writer or readers, and make use of this volume as a humble part of that mighty instrumentality, which He is now employing, to bring back this lost world again to Him.

## Hymn of Thanksgiving.

FOR the blessings of the field,
　For the stores the gardens
　　yield,
For the vine's exalted juice,
For the generous olive's use;

Flocks that whiten all the plain,
Yellow sheaves of ripened grain,
Clouds that drop their fattening
　dews,
Suns that temperate warmth diffuse;

All that Spring, with bounteous
　hand,
Scatters o'er the smiling land;
All that liberal Autumn pours
From her rich o'erflowing stores;

These to Thee, my God, we owe—
Source whence all our blessings
　flow!
And for these my soul shall raise
Grateful vows and solemn praise.

Yet should rising whirlwinds tear
From its stem the ripening ear,
Should the fig-tree's blasted shoot
Drop her green untimely fruit—

Should the vine put forth no more,
Nor the olive yield her store,
Though the sickening flocks should fall,
And the herds desert the stall—

Should thine altered hand restrain
The early and the latter rain,
Blast each opening bud of joy,
And the rising year destroy—

Yet to Thee my soul should raise
Grateful vows and solemn praise,
And, when every blessing's flown,
Love Thee—for Thyself alone.

ANNA LŒTITIA BARBAULD.